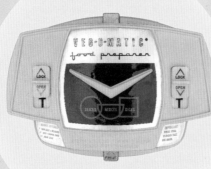

But, Wait! There's More!

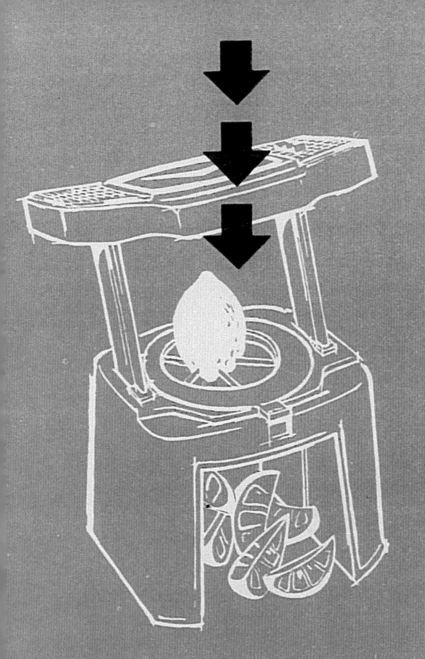

PEARS

EGGS

APPLES

LEMONS

RADISH ROSE

Center radish, on wedger blades, then press to ¾ depth, withdraw and immerse in cold water until petals open.

But, Wait! There's More!

THE IRRESISTIBLE

APPEAL AND SPIEL

OF RONCO AND POPEIL

TIMOTHY SAMUELSON

RIZZOLI
NEW YORK

First published in the United States of America

in 2002 by

RIZZOLI INTERNATIONAL PUBLICATIONS, INC.

300 Park Avenue South

New York, NY 10010

ISBN: 0-8478-2431-4

LC: 2001093681

Distributed by St. Martin's Press

Printed and bound in Hong Kong

Illustration Credits

Unless noted here, all photographs of original product graphics and commercials belonging to the author are by David R. Phillips. Permission to reproduce graphic materials and commercial excerpts was granted through the courtesy of Ronald M. Popeil.

Page 25: photograph of Ron Popeil and Mel Korey courtesy of the National Housewares Manufacturers Association; **62–63**: film of Veg-O-Matic commercial courtesy of MacDonald & Associates, Chicago; **70**: Portable Sewing Machine graphic courtesy of John S. Doyel; **74**: film of Spray Gun commercial courtesy of MacDonald & Associates, Chicago; **78**: Auto Cup graphic courtesy of John S. Doyel; **79**: Sit-On Trash Compactor graphic courtesy of Pamela Popeil; **86**: film of London Aire commercial courtesy of MacDonald & Associates, Chicago; **107**: film of Pocket Fisherman commercial courtesy of MacDonald & Associates, Chicago; **128**: photograph of Timothy Samuelson by Paul Natkin.

Stuffed Dill Pickle—Cut pickle in half—insert serrated cutter over soft core. Twist gently, at same time pushing forward. When cutter is completely embedded, insert a knife through back end of cutter and twist to remove soft core. Stuff with cream cheese—serve sliced.

Fancy Cookies, Fancy Jellied Cranberry Slices, Fancy Cucumber Slices, Scalloped Potatoes, Fancy Melon Slices—Just press out with Fancy Cutter—Foods will be attractively shaped with neat clean scalloped edges.

Contents

Scalloped and Cored Grapefruit—Halve a grapefruit. Using corer form a continuous scalloped edge around grapefruit. Center corer over grapefruit core and twist back and forth, pressing lightly. When corer touches bottom, pry slightly, core will lift out.

Fancy Canapes—Cover slices of bread with lunch meat, cheese, caviar or spreads. Press fancy cutter through bread, then with slight twisting action lift canape. To release canape from fancy cutter push out with finger.

Author's Preface

When I first became interested in Popeil and Ronco products, my instinct was to keep that interest to myself. As curator of architecture and design for the Chicago Historical Society, anything I do reflects on the dignity and reputation of one of Chicago's most respected cultural institutions. What would people think if they learned of my secret fascination with television-advertised gizmos with names that ended in "O-Matic?"

Was it a risky, career-destroying stretch to take the Popeil story seriously? In actuality, the story was perfectly compatible with my work. The essence of Chicago's rapid growth from mud hole to modern metropolis was largely the result of creative hustlers whose unconventional efforts to make a fast buck resulted in genuine achievement. This same free-for-all environment gave creative architects and designers the freedom to create everything from skyscrapers to chewing-gum wrappers in new forms that caught the attention of the world.

Such was the case with the Popeil family, whose clever household products entered the public consciousness by forging a unity between the pitch of the street vendor and the technology of television broadcasting. An equally important, yet often overlooked, part of the story is the fact that most of the products were exceptionally well designed, combining beauty and utility in the best traditions of architect Louis Sullivan's oft-quoted dictum, "form follows function."

My personal interest in all things Popeil started about eight years ago, when a visit to a resale store yielded a 1950s' plastic donut maker which embodied an uncommon blend of beauty, utility, and ease of manufacture—all the key hallmarks of good industrial design. The box identified the maker as "Popeil Brothers," the same name that I recalled from all those intense television advertisements that I had known since childhood. This simple $1 plastic gadget led me to take a fresh look at the entire line of products manufactured by Popeil Brothers and Ronco, most of which proved to possess a similar integrity of design and technology.

I freely confess that I found the Popeil and Ronco commercials to be extremely annoying when I first saw them, but I guess they finally won me over. Years after the commercials aired, I found myself searching thrift stores and online auctions for long-out-of-production items. Even though many of the products are over forty years old and made of seemingly vulnerable plastic, almost all still do their intended jobs well. In many cases I try to find two of each product—one for study and research, and one for my everyday use. Veg-O-Matics, Chop-O-Matics, and other plastic gizmos sit in peaceful coexistence with the "less is more" discipline of my Ludwig Mies van der Rohe–designed apartment. Occupants of neighboring units probably little suspect that the low hum emanating from my apartment in the morning is from a genuine 1978 Ronco Inside-the-Shell Egg Scrambler whipping up breakfast.

In this book, I have made no attempt to list each and every product ever made by Popeil Brothers and Ronco. I'm more than happy to leave that niche open for those inclined toward writing books for avid collectors. The products represented in this book are the ones that I feel are most representative for telling the overall story or, in some cases, are simply my personal favorites.

The secret's out about my passion for Popeil and Ronco products—but I guess it's not a bad thing after all. My years of dealing with the intricate nuances of Chicago history and the likes of Louis Sullivan and Frank Lloyd Wright was never good material for casual cocktail party conversation and usually attracted only the polite interest of a small circle of like-minded zealots. Nowadays, people actually come up to me and ask about my latest Popeil research. With minimal resistance, I'll oblige requests to recite the lines of the classic Veg-O-Matic television commercial.

It was only on rare occasions that I'd get requests from the media to comment on issues regarding history, architecture, and design. To my amazement and disbelief, ever since my Popeil research was "outed," my message book became filled with inquiries from some of the biggest names of the broadcast and print media. You can imagine my surprise and anticipation when a senior editor from the prestigious publishing house of Rizzoli International Publications left a message saying that she wanted to discuss doing a book project with me. "Ah-ha!" I thought, "after all my years of research, she must want a book on Louis Sullivan or some lofty book on architecture or design."

She didn't. You'll *never* guess what she *did* want!

—Timothy Samuelson

ANOTHER

GREAT POPEIL PRODUCT

®

Introduction

Everyone knows the Popeil family and their "amazing" products. It would be difficult not to. For over forty years, the Popeils' high-energy television commercials have made them familiar intruders into America's living rooms. Chances are, your own home—or those of your friends and family—bears evidence of their seductive visits. Countless Veg-O-Matics, Kitchen Magicians, Miracle Brooms, and other gadgets sit tucked away in America's cupboards, giving silent testimony to the power of the family's broadcast salesmanship. Even if you stoically resisted the temptation to buy, their commercials and products are probably nevertheless indelibly stored in your mind.

The Popeil story is a classic tale of hustle and chutzpah. In the beginning, Samuel J. Popeil and his brother, Raymond, started as street pitchmen, demonstrating inexpensive household items at beachfront boardwalks and county fairs in the 1930s and 1940s. With only a table, a simple kitchen gadget, and a mesmerizing incantation of voice and body language, they had the uncanny ability to stop strangers in their tracks and get them to eagerly pull out money for something they initially had no intention of buying.

The Popeils later adapted these same skills to the emerging medium of television advertising, establishing what was to become the basis of their fame and success. Spellbinding sales pitches that worked on the street proved to work even better on the small screen: People saw the products on television and felt compelled to go out and buy them.

The products themselves are a key part of the Popeil success story. Most were clever kitchen gadgets invented by Samuel J. Popeil and manufactured in the Popeil Brothers factory under Raymond's watchful eye. Simple to manufacture and inexpensive to sell, the products became larger than life under the lens of Popeil–style promotions. With names like "Kitchen Magician" or "Chop-O-Matic," they conveyed a sense of power and efficiency. Breathlessly spoken descriptions were laced with words like "miracle" and "magic" and often punctuated with the now-famous question, "Isn't that amazing?"

The story continues today with the ongoing television presence of Ron Popeil, Samuel J. Popeil's son, who has earned popular culture immortality as the greatest television pitchman of them all. Like his father, Ron Popeil became a master live-demonstration pitchman at an early age, eventually moving to television in 1964 to sell his own line of products under the name Ronco. Commercials for products like Mr. Microphone, the Inside-the-Shell Egg Scrambler, and the Showtime Rotisserie have become classics of the genre and were major influences in shaping the present-day advertising phenomena known as the infomercial. At any hour of the day, it is still possible to see television advertisements that give a tip of the hat to the Popeils and their amazing spiels.

But underneath the layers of promotional hype, the Popeil products are true devices of ingenuity and utility and—sometimes—even beauty. Each was created with the simple goal of improving everyday life at a price everyone could afford.

To accomplish this, the Popeils used an instinctive grasp of physics, technology, and materials to create deceptively simple objects that often made people wonder "Why didn't I think of that?" In other instances they created innovative products that people never knew they needed—but came to feel they did as a result of the Popeils' persuasive advertising.

An unexpected facet of Popeil and Ronco products was the unusually high quality of their product designs. Visually attractive and modern in styling, they were artistically expressive of the versatile possibilities of plastics and other emerging materials of the latter twentieth century. In fact, many of the products can rightfully take their place with some of the classic contemporary designs of the time in which they were created. While striking in design, the products were simultaneously conceived to facilitate fast and inexpensive manufacturing.

Today, the name "Popeil" has joined with that of cartoonist Rube Goldberg as a popular synonym for "gadget." The Popeil legacy has been escalated to even greater fame as the perennial subject of countless jokes and parodies, and it frequently emerges in the course of everyday conversation. Whether remembered with fond nostalgia or roll-of-the-eyes bemusement, the Popeils clearly have talked their way into the arena of American popular culture.

Perhaps inventing and pitching goods was in their genes, for it seemed that the Popeil family was predestined to make and sell items in unconventional ways.

Samuel Joseph Popeil was born in New York City on January 22, 1915, the son of Isidore and Mary Popeil, both children of Polish Jewish immigrant families. Isidore Popeil worked in New York City's garment district, where he held the position of cutter, a skilled job that required shrewd judgment to know how to cut a bolt of cloth to yield the maximum number of pieces of clothing. If Samuel Popeil's later successes in business and manufacturing can be attributed to handed-down family influences, his father's skills in the clothing trade certainly may have been a factor. Nevertheless, his strongest influence undoubtedly came from his mother's family, the Morrises of Asbury Park, New Jersey, a popular resort community. The Morris family was a virtual dynasty of salesmen and manufacturers who used their skills and street smarts to succeed in the field of live-demonstration merchandising—a profession whose practitioners are most commonly known as "pitchmen."

Several of Mary Popeil's brothers and in-laws were successful professional pitchmen, each possessing the ability to stand in a public place and sell products to the passing crowd by nuances of voice, gesture, and word. Most of the extended Morris

ABOVE: **His street pitching days long behind him, Samuel J. Popeil posed for this portrait (ca. 1970) as a successful millionaire.**

OPPOSITE: **This 1937 postcard depicts the recreational attractions of Asbury Park, New Jersey, including the oceanfront boardwalk that served as the pitchman's training ground for Samuel and Raymond Popeil.**

family polished their pitching skills on Asbury Park's oceanfront boardwalk. One of the legends of the boardwalk was Mary's brother Nathan "Nat" Morris, whose intense hard-sell techniques generated sales to the extent that he was later able to establish small factories to manufacture small kitchen gadgets to supply other pitchmen. Mary's other brothers, Abe and Joe, also proved their own mastery of the pitch profession, as did the husbands of her sisters, Esther and Molly. Esther's husband, Irving Rosenbloom, also established his own manufacturing business, producing early plastic kitchenware in the 1940s; he later became the owner of a successful toy company.

Growing up in New York City, Samuel Popeil only had occasional contact with the world of pitch and promotion practiced by his mother's family. But this changed in 1932 when he was seventeen, and it altered his life forever. His uncle Irving Rosenbloom had become ill and was unable to do a scheduled demonstration of a kitchen gadget at a branch of Macy's in New York. Samuel was asked to replace him. In an interview given over forty years later, he recalled with trepidation his live-demonstration debut: "It was an ordeal. I had never spoken before an audience before, and I cut my finger pretty badly."

Despite his awkward start, Samuel Popeil discovered that he had a natural ability to pitch. Under the tutelage of his uncles, he successfully perfected the art. One of his best teachers was Nat Morris, who not only imparted the nuances of his successful pitch technique, but also conveyed the value of manufacturing his own products, thereby eliminating middleman's costs.

Pitchmen and the World of Knives

Knives with super-sharp cutting prowess have been a staple of live and television pitchmen for decades. The most famous of these, the Ginsu, has no Popeil connection, although Popeil Brothers still had considerable experience in selling knives. Most pitchmen's knives—including the Ginsu—came from the Qwikut Company of Fremont, Ohio, manufacturers of serrated knives that could cut a can in half yet still slice a tomato paper-thin. Popeil Brothers repackaged and distributed similar knives under the names Feather Touch and Hi Temp, promoting them with demonstrations that included sawing through a leather boot or cutting through a nail. In 1976, Popeil Brothers introduced a serrated knife with a foldable cutting board promoted as the Bionic Knife. The name was allegedly Samuel Popeil's sly response to gossip that son Ron Popeil was romantically involved with Lindsay Wagner, star of The Bionic Woman, at the time.

Important - Please Read Carefully

I am made of glass, and will not stain or discolor; therefore I am clean, stainless, sanitary and odorless. Please take special care of me and I will give you many years of service. I am as keen as a razor, ideal for slicing tomatoes, oranges, lemons, grapefruit, and especially constructed for separating the meaty parts of grapefruit from its rind. I will not punch a hole through the rind. It is important that I only be used on a soft wooden board, avoid metal or porcelain; after all I am only made of glass. When I am not in use put me back in the box or keep me away from your silverware. Because I cannot be exchanged for any reason, the manufacturer, distributor, or retailer cannot be held responsible for my actions.

IDEAL FOR CAKE, PIES MERINGUE AND BANANAS

I will make an ideal bridge prize and I am sure your dear friends or neighbors will be delighted with my services. If you would like my twin the price is very reasonable. Write to my agent and distributor, referred to below.

Agents and distributors of all sorts, wholesale and retail, special prices in one half or dozen lots for bridges and favors. Booklet sent on request.

Samuel and Raymond Popeil hawked their Uncle Irving Rosenbloom's Vitex glass knife at the 1939 New York World's Fair. Their Uncle Nat Morris also distributed his own glass knife, accompanied by quaintly worded instructions printed on tissue paper that doubled as packing material.

NEW YORK WORLD'S FAIR

THE NEW Vitex-Glas KNIFE

Always
SHARP
SANITARY
STAINLESS

The Depression era proved to be one of the most fertile periods for live-demonstration salesmen. In a period when money was scarce, their seductive pitches gave the public a rare opportunity to purchase an affordable new appliance that seemingly would make everyday life easier. While still in high school, Samuel Popeil spent most of his spare time selling products through his newfound pitching skills. The products were simple kitchen gadgets—mostly knives, graters, and peelers—purchased wholesale from suppliers or obtained from his uncles. To expand his business, he trained some of his school friends to pitch products on a percentage basis. By the time he graduated, he had a half dozen of his classmates working on his behalf.

Samuel's most adept student proved to be his younger brother, Raymond, who was born in 1921. He later recalled that Raymond was "so proficient that in his grip even the dullest knife was transformed into an indispensable kitchen utensil." Through his graceful hand movements, Raymond made whatever he demonstrated look easy to use. In fact, even many years later, during the Popeils' successful advertising campaigns on television, it was Raymond's steady hands and arms—carefully shaved for good appearance—that effortlessly demonstrated the products on most of their commercials.

The secret of Popeil Brothers' success was to buy large quantities of goods at low wholesale prices, and resell them via the magical allure of their well-honed demonstration pitches. Although the profit margin on each item was small—often under $1—the number of items that were repeatedly sold to ever-changing crowds of twenty-five to fifty people every ten or fifteen minutes resulted in considerable cash. The brothers soon found that they were making more money by demonstrating products than their father, Isidore, was after years of experience in the clothing industry.

One of Samuel and Raymond's early sales products was a solid glass knife that was promoted as always being sanitary and sharp. They received their knives from Nat Morris and Irving Rosenbloom, who also sold the knives themselves and to other pitchmen. At the 1939 New York World's Fair, Samuel and Raymond were among a dozen demonstrators strategically placed around the fairgrounds to pitch the glass knife, and other crowd-attracting products, such as spiral slicers and patented fruit juice extractors.

His pitching career on a quick ascent, Samuel Popeil married Julia Schwartz while still in his teens. The household expanded with the birth of two children, Jerome in 1933, and Ronald in 1935. But the marriage soon resulted in separation and divorce. Young Jerome and Ronald were placed in a New York state boarding.school, and later went to live with grandparents Isidore and Mary in Florida, which resulted in their losing contact with their parents for much of their early childhood. Soon after America's entry into World War II, the Popeil brothers' sales partnership was temporarily disbanded when Raymond entered the service, leaving Samuel to reassess his life and career.

Seeking a fresh start, Samuel Popeil left New York and moved to Chicago in 1942. Although his personal problems were probably a major factor in his decision to relocate, there were sound business reasons as well. As a centrally located transportation hub, Chicago offered easy access to the countless county fairs and other public events that took place throughout the rural Midwest; in other words, Chicago was the perfect place for a professional pitchman.

Chicago also offered the attraction of the Maxwell Street Market, a raucous outdoor affair that attracted the urban poor and newly arrived immigrants with its array of goods aggressively proffered with the promise of a bargain. At Maxwell Street, skilled pitchmen lined up almost side-by-side to vie for the attention of the passing crowds, competing not only among themselves, but also with the market's ever-present noise and activity. There, as in New York, Samuel Popeil resold gadgets he purchased wholesale from various manufacturers and distributors, including products manufactured by his uncles back east. He trained a new staff of demonstrators from the ranks of out-of-work Chicago actors and, as he later said, "anyone else with an extroverted personality."

He also experimented with creating gadgets of his own, taking advantage of Chicago's reputation as a manufacturing center. According to his cousin, Arnold Morris, two of Samuel Popeil's first products were a small platform slicer with an adjustable blade and his version of the glass knife. His uncles were chagrined to discover that some of these early products were copies of their own wares. In the end, the adaptation proved to be merely an example of the back-and-forth "borrowing" of products between the Morris and the Popeil families that continued for decades, sometimes resulting in fierce inner-family lawsuits. When talking with family members today, though, it is often unclear who really originated many of the products.

176—Maxwell Street, Chicago

ABOVE: **This 1941 postcard shows Chicago's Maxwell Street Market as Samuel J. Popeil would have found it upon his arrival in Chicago, although the image in no way conveys the scope of the scene's crowds, noise, and smells.**
OPPOSITE: **Touted as "the instrument that will thrill you," Uncle Nat Morris' Metric Vegetable Slicer was a staple for post-World War II pitchman, including aspiring actor and broadcaster Ed McMahon, who once hawked it on the boardwalks.**

At the end of his wartime service, Raymond Popeil joined Samuel in Chicago. Resuming their business relationship, they decided to follow the example of their uncle Nat and establish their own manufacturing business. By late 1945, the brothers had rented space in an old loft on the northern edge of downtown Chicago and established the firm of Popeil Brothers, a business dedicated to the manufacture and sale of small kitchen gadgets.

Drawing from their own experiences as live-demonstration pitchmen, they manufactured inexpensive products for wholesale to professional demonstrators as well as retail stores. Popeil Brothers initially employed its own staff of demonstrators to sell their products at fairs and markets, but as their reputation as a wholesale demonstrator's supply house increased, the firm's dependence on its own staff of demonstrators gradually diminished, eventually disappearing altogether.

Throughout its thirty-four-year history, Popeil Brothers retained its identity as a family-run, no-nonsense business that had its origins in the tough, streetwise world of the public marketplace. Both brothers ran the business with a gruff demeanor and an emphasis on frugality, practicality, and profit. Even decades later, in 1969, when Popeil Brothers became a successful publicly traded corporation, the firm's executive offices remained unglamorous and within their factory, where every detail of its operations were under Samuel and Raymond Popeil's constant scrutiny.

The Art of the Pitch

It takes a special kind of person to stand up in front of a crowd at a county fair—or in front of a television camera—and convince complete strangers to spend money on a product that they initially had no intention of buying. Being successful in the "pitch" business required salesmanship, showmanship, and an understanding of human psychology—skills the Popeil family had in spades and which were exemplified by their enormous, well-remembered, and much-imitated success.

Practitioners of the art of verbal sales are often referred to as "pitchmen," a generic, gender-specific term that unfortunately obscures the fact that many women also had successful careers in this line of work. Some experts argue that the term "pitchman" refers specifically to the process of selling by the power of voice and that people who talk while operating a product are called "demonstrators." In the trade, however, the differentiation between the two terms has become blurred, and they are often used interchangeably.

One of the most attractive advantages to being a pitchman was that start-up and overhead costs were low, making it affordable for anyone to be in business for themselves. Many found being a pitchman an accessible way to start their own businesses, while others saw it as a lucrative way of making extra money in their spare time. Countless struggling students worked their way through school by pitching products, and actors were especially adept in using their theatrical skills to pitch products between jobs. A notable pitch alumnus is television personality Ed McMahon, who funded his education by selling Nat Morris's "Morris Metric Slicer" on the Atlantic City boardwalk.

Making a living by doing live-demonstration selling is not an easy profession. It involves hard work, long hours, and personal stamina—not to mention a strong voice. It is not easy to stand at a table all day long—often in all kinds of weather—and give a high-energy pitch over and over again.

The classic demonstration pitch is skillfully meted out in stages to build interest and curiosity, and ends with a persuasive "turn," where the pitchman gets the audience to put out their money for the product. Although variations on the pitch are as infinite as the individual skills and personalities of the people who practice the art, there are common techniques that most live-demonstration pitches—and pitch-derived television commercials—have in common:

LOCATION, LOCATION, LOCATION: When doing a live-demonstration pitch, strategically locating the sales booth can be an important factor for success. For example, whenever Ron Popeil sold kitchenware at county fairs and public events, he located his booth near the women's restrooms so he could be assured of a captive and potentially receptive audience. Similarly, when demonstrating kitchenware at drugstores and dime stores, he stayed close to the makeup aisle. When selecting time for airing television commercials, similar strategies were devised to match the product with the appropriate viewing audience.

BUILD A CROWD AND HOLD 'EM: The first challenge for a live-demonstration pitchman is to build a crowd. Doing so begins by attracting one or two people and getting them to stop and listen, thereby creating the "seed" for a larger audience. The sight of the first people standing in rapt attention piques the curiosity of others passing by and encourages them to stop, too. A good demonstrator can often generate a crowd of fifty or more people within the first few minutes. As the crowd builds, the new arrivals lock in the earlier spectators, making it difficult for them to leave.

MAKE THE PRODUCT SOUND AND LOOK INDISPENSABLE: With enthusiastic nuances of voice and gesture, the successful pitchman convinces the audience that the product makes an everyday task easier or provides a completely new service. In addition to its main function, the ideal pitchman's product is one that can do more than one task, giving extra value to the customer, such as Popeil's Food Glamorizer ("Does the work of a whole drawerful of appliances!"). The presentation is given while flawlessly operating the product itself. As Samuel Popeil once observed: "Making anything look easy is half the battle. If you're clumsy, the customer will walk away."

SAY IT AGAIN—AND AGAIN: During the course of a pitch, the usefulness of the product is usually demonstrated and described multiple times with slight variances to build customer interest and enthusiasm. On television, important points were often flashed across the screen in bold white lettering.

THE AMAZING WORLD OF SUPERLATIVES: A seasoned pitchman generously uses superlatives to describe a product. Frequently used terms include: "magic," "miracle," "fantastic," and "amazing," among a multitude of others. These descriptions figure prominently in television pitch-style advertisements, and often appear on the product's packaging.

GET THE AUDIENCE INVOLVED: While making the pitch, the demonstrator takes special notice of audience members who respond by nodding their heads or showing other outward signs of interest. Not only do rhetorical questions like "Isn't that amazing?" cause people to visibly respond, but they also serve as a catalyst to get other audience members involved, too. The pitchman also spikes audience attention by throwing in an occasional joke ("...chops chicken for chicken salad, ham for ham salad, horse for horseradish...").

ASKING FOR THE MONEY—"THE TURN": A cardinal rule for both live and television demonstrations is that the price is never revealed until the end of the pitch. As audience interest in the product is fanned during the demonstration, a feeling of suspense is created by not revealing the price. The act of revealing the price is in itself a subtle art of the demonstration profession—a technique known in the trade as "the turn." Every demonstrator has his or her own variations in executing "the turn," but there are many common ways to do it.

Five or ten minutes into the pitch, the demonstrator suddenly says, "You're probably asking yourself what this product costs." The demonstrator explains that the product is soon to be introduced in a nationwide campaign and will be sold for a retail price that is typically a hard-sounding round number like "ten dollars." The demonstrator then adds that "it's well worth it for all the wonderful things it does." And this statement is followed up by a "special offer" for the day, a figure like $3.98 or $7.77. The odd number gives the impression of a true bargain—a psychological sales technique commonly used in modern retailing. Many products pack-

aged especially for the pitch trade have the "retail" price printed in large numbers on the box, giving a highly visible assurance to even those farthest away in the crowd that they are being offered a "bargain."

Variations include "the countdown," a suspense-building technique in which the price is progressively reduced from the "suggested retail" price. ("You won't have to pay ten dollars for this product...you won't even have to pay seven dollars...or five dollars.... In this special offer, you can have it for the low, low price of $3.98.") Some demonstrators imply that the price is a "limited time offer" or that the product will be offered "one to a family" because "supplies are limited." This sets up a feeling of competition amongst the spectators, making people want to rush forward with their money for fear of being left out of the deal. This uncontrollable desire to buy spreads like wildfire throughout the crowd.

BUT, WAIT! THERE'S MORE!: THE BONUS PRODUCT: Before taking money from the already eager crowd, many demonstrators will suddenly produce another smaller product—sometimes using the legendary line "But, wait! There's more!" The pitchman will then do a brief demonstration of the new product, showing its usefulness and versatility. Following classic techniques of "the turn," the "suggested retail" price for the new gadget is revealed at the end of the demonstration. Instead of offering the new product at a discounted price, the demonstrator astounds the crowd by offering to give it away free with the purchase of the other product. In some instances, the "special" price is lowered even further, or additional "free" items are added. The astonished spectators can't believe their good fortune and are eager to buy.

YOUR MONEY BACK—NO QUESTIONS ASKED: Live-demonstration pitchmen rarely made "satisfaction-guaranteed-or-your-money-back" offers since both the seller and the buyer knew that they would probably never see each other again. Money-back guarantees were freely offered at the end of television pitches as a way of making prospective customers think they had nothing to lose by buying the product. Not only did television pitchmen promise that the item could be returned "no questions asked," they also often invited customers to keep any accompanying bonus cookbooks or small gadgets as a gift for their trouble. In reality, television pitchmen knew that only a small percentage of dissatisfied customers ever bothered to ask for a refund.

The demonstrator is now ready to take the money from the eager crowd. To make buyers even more enthusiastic, demonstrators often create a sense of competition among the crowd by holding up the money that was collected and pointing out customers ready to buy, exclaiming, "He wants one! She wants one! That man over there wants one!"

The money is then taken from all but the last few people in line, to whom the demonstrator says, "Hold on—there's something else I want to show you." These already willing buyers become the seed audience for attracting a new crowd, and the process starts all over again.

Nevertheless, the Popeils' aggressive emphasis on frugality and profit was never at the expense of the products and its purchasers. Typical of a family-run business, there was always a sense of pride and accountability associated with each Popeil Brothers product. Even though the products were usually promoted with hype and hyperbole, they almost always did what they were supposed to do and were intended to give years of good value to the purchaser.

Tough talking, cigar smoking Samuel Popeil was the most visible representative of the company. He had a special talent for thinking up unusual gadgets that could attract attention whether sold on a street corner or sitting on a store shelf. Equally important, the products could be manufactured and sold at a modest cost. When asked, Samuel usually denied being an inventor, describing himself instead as a "tinkerer, an improviser, somebody who fiddles with existing products and makes them better." Raymond Popeil not only contributed his sales and promotional talents but also proved to be a skilled manager of manufacturing and distribution operations. He usually kept a low public profile, but was still called upon to reprise his old pitchman's skills to demonstrate a product for prospective customers. Finally, to keep the business a family affair, Isidore Popeil was persuaded to leave Florida and come to Chicago to help run the factory. He brought with him Samuel's young sons, Jerome and Ronald, who spent much of their out-of-school time assembling and packaging products at the factory. After the divorce, the boys' mother disappeared from their lives, and Samuel was too preoccupied with building the business to be an active father. Even while living in Chicago, Jerome and Ronald continued to live with their grandparents and seldom saw their father.

Most of the earliest Popeil products were small metal kitchen hand appliances like graters and spiral slicers, which retailed for a dollar or less. The metal parts were fabricated by other companies, but assembled and packaged at the Popeil Brothers factory. By the late 1940s, Popeil Brothers began to specialize in making plastic versions of traditional metal kitchen utensils, such as flour sifters, cookie presses, and storage canisters. In their plastic products, Popeil Brothers used the inherent qualities of the material to create products that were not only pleasing to the eye, but that were also inexpensive to manufacture and sell.

In addition to plastics, television changed the nature of business for both Popeil Brothers and the pitchmen during the 1950s. In 1950, three million American households had televisions; by 1955, thirty-four million did. As television gained popularity, it diverted the public's attention from popular pastimes like movies, dancing, and bowling, and also threatened the fairs, carnivals, and other public events that were the bread and butter of live-demonstration pitchmen. But just as a seasoned pitchman knows how to pick the best spot to attract crowds at a county fair, so did the pitchman's profession recognize television as an ideal medium to reach even greater audiences.

The operators of the early television stations needed the services of the pitchmen as much as the pitchmen needed television. To make television a financial success, broadcasters had to find advertisers to support their programming. During the previous decades, radio had evolved successful and sophisticated methods of broadcast advertising, but the emerging medium of television needed advertisers who could sell by sight as well as sound.

Pitchmen were the perfect people to fill this need. Soon, the airwaves were filled with televised versions of pitches that had been staples of fairs, dime stores, and boardwalks for years—an endless parade of clever kitchen gadgets, miracle automobile waxes, medicines, and elixirs. Popeil Brothers enjoyed considerable success by supplying goods wholesale to many of the pioneering television pitchmen, but did not produce filmed commercials of their own until 1961.

Yet a prophetic brush with the new medium came in 1956 when the Grant Company—a Chicago firm specializing in selling products on television—selected Popeil Brothers' newly released Chop-O-Matic food chopper for one of its pitch-style television promotions. For the on-air pitchman, the Grant Company chose a young man who had great success in demonstrating the Chop-O-Matic at Woolworth's in downtown Chicago—Samuel Popeil's twenty-one-year-old son, Ronald.

Although Ron Popeil had kept his distance from his father and uncle's company, and years of separation had created tension between father and son, their careers followed quite similar paths. Just as his father had discovered his talents as a pitchman in his late teens, so too did Ron Popeil. At the age of sixteen, Popeil first encountered Chicago's raucous Maxwell Street Market, where he closely observed the techniques of the seasoned demonstrators. When Ron tried pitching himself, he proved to be excellent at it.

I created a monster. Everyone tried to imitate our television marketing. Because of that, the demand for TV time is so great that spots that we used to buy for $200 to $300 cost seven to ten times that much.

—Samuel J. Popeil, 1979

While still in his teens, Ron Popeil established himself as a skilled pitchman, working the circuit of county fairs, trade shows, and the Maxwell Street Market. On weekdays, he pitched his products at Woolworth's. The Chop-O-Matic was one of the many products that he regularly demonstrated there, delivering his pitch with a firmly paced, yet personable delivery. Young and handsome, he was especially popular with the store's female shoppers, many of whom returned day after day to spend their lunch hours watching him demonstrate.

By the time he was selected to do the Grant Company commercial, Ron Popeil had perfected his presentation of the Chop-O-Matic. The resulting commercial was essentially a filmed version of his standard live presentation, a four-minute, unscripted pitch showing him standing at a table and intensely yet affably showing the value and versatility of the gadget—despite the fact that the loud pounding of the Chop-O-Matic all but drowned out Ron's voice at different points during his spiel.

The presentation was filled with attention-grabbing, superlative-laced descriptions and repetitive mention of the product's usefulness. It ended with the classic price-revealing pitchman's "turn" (see page 18), complete with the promise of a discounted price and a bonus cookbook, *50 Secret Recipes by World Famous Chefs*. Several decades later, Ron Popeil recalled in his autobiography, "In all candor, I really don't remember where all those famous chefs came from."

This modest commercial put Ron Popeil before American households for the first time. Although his father and uncle's firm had no direct financial stake in making the commercial, they nevertheless reaped the bounty of television promotion.

The Chop-O-Matics sold as fast as the Popeil Brothers factory could make them, for they appealed to the television-viewing families of the era who were pursuing the American dream of having a modern home equipped with labor-saving appliances. For those who could not afford a $40 electric blender, a versatile $3.98 hand-operated food chopper offered on television was an accessible alternative. When the product was presented by a seasoned pitchman, the buyer could be convinced that the $3.98 chopper was just as good as, if not better than, its expensive electric counterpart. They could be satisfied—even if momentarily—that they were advancing one step closer to achieving success in their lives.

Initially, following the Chop-O-Matic ad, Ron Popeil made no further commercials and returned to demonstrating at Woolworth's and on the fair circuit. For their part, Samuel and Raymond Popeil were astounded by the sales that were generated by the Grant Company's Chop-O-Matic television promotion. To keep the momentum going, they decided to concentrate on manufacturing the Chop-O-Matic and other products that would be suitable for promoting the same way, although they still had no interest in making their own television commercials, preferring instead to wholesale their products directly to television marketers.

Eventually, though, they realized that if they were going to be successful in selling their products on television, they were going to have to make the commercials themselves. In 1961, they launched their first independent venture in television advertising—auspiciously choosing as their first promotion a new product that came to be indelibly associated with their name and fame—the Veg-O-Matic.

Unlike many of Samuel J. Popeil's earlier creations, which were adaptations of existing products, the Veg-O-Matic was an original concept—a reverse guillotine for food. Vegetables or other firm foodstuffs were placed atop a round grid of sharpened blades that were mounted atop a small plastic platform. By briskly pressing down on a spring-loaded overhead plunger, the food was pushed through the sharpened steel blades and transformed into perfect uniform slices. With a slight adjustment of its blade rings, the Veg-O-Matic could make thick or thin slices, dice, and make French fries.

ABOVE: **The merging of beauty, utility, and ease of manufacture made Popeil Brothers'
1950 plastic Donut Maker a classic of product design.**
OPPOSITE: **Early Popeil Brothers products were largely retailed to attract female homemakers, but
wholesaling was clearly directed to a predominantly male market. Potential wholesale customers visiting
the Popeil Brothers booth at the 1953 National Housewares Show in Chicago were provided with a souvenir
8 x 10" glossy photograph of the tiny-aproned "Miss Kitchen Gadget" as a sales incentive.**

Promotion of the Veg-O-Matic established a new Popeil Brothers marketing strategy that the company followed closely for most of its subsequent products. The filmed television commercial was produced and paid for by Popeil Brothers and provided free of charge to their network of distributors who were encouraged to air it on behalf of the retail stores to whom they supplied products or to sell the product directly on television. Popeil Brothers made money from the increased wholesale orders resulting from the product's television exposure. The initial investment in making the commercial was more than repaid.

The Veg-O-Matic television ad was an abbreviated version of a classic street pitchman's presentation and showed only the agile arms and hands of Raymond Popeil as he deftly demonstrated all the various tasks the Veg-O-Matic could perform. While Raymond worked, the announcer gave a rapid-fire commentary of the slicer's usefulness and utility, punctuated by now-familiar phrases like "Isn't that amazing?" Also, just as with a street pitch, the price of the item was not revealed until the very end of the spiel—the alliterative, bargain sounding price of $9.95 (later sold for the even more alliterative $7.77)—followed by the offer of a free recipe booklet.

The rapid-fire presentation that is popularly associated with the Veg-O-Matic commercial was a result of necessity rather than choice. New Federal Communications Commission (FCC) regulations limited the length of television commercials to two minutes or less—a marked reduction from Ron Popeil's four-minute 1956 pitch for the Chop-O-Matic. Knowing the importance of the classic pitch, the Popeils were hesitant to abbreviate it to make the commercial fit into its time limit. The only alternative was to speed up the pace at which the pitch was delivered.

Even while pitched at an unprecedented speed, the Veg-O-Matic promotion was an unqualified success—over 11 million units were ultimately sold. The basic precedent upon which the

Veg-O-Matic was created and marketed was repeated for a succession of products that came from the Popeil Brothers' factory throughout the 1960s and 1970s. Initially, most were hand-operated plastic kitchen gadgets that sold for under $10—many of which were variations on the familiar "O-Matic" name. By the late 1960s, the firm began cautiously branching out into non-kitchen items, such as the 1967 Steamset, a women's hair curler set, and the Trimcomb, a home-barbering kit. Another change in marketing came with the introduction of the Pocket Fisherman in 1972, one of Popeil Brothers' best-selling and now most nostalgically remembered products; its success inspired a small line of fishing-related Popeil products, but none achieved the success of the original.

Although the Popeil products were of good quality, it was the commercials that garnered them fame. After the success of the Veg-O-Matic, Popeil Brothers put special emphasis on creating their distinctive brand of television advertising, carefully polishing each pitch in their own in-factory rehearsal room before doing the studio filming. Despite the Popeil's mastery of the art of salesmanship, the complexities of creating television commercials prompted them to hire Bill Samuels, an experienced advertising man, to oversee their productions. Samuels also happened to be an accomplished hypnotist—although it's difficult to speculate on whether this fact had any impact on the commercials.

No dishes to wash!
For kids who don't like egg whites!
Makes health foods, shakes, eggnogs, gourmet sauces & gravies taste better!
Try pre-blended hard-boiled eggs!
Great for camping!
—Box for Inside-the-Shell Egg Scrambler, 1978

The main point of the television commercials was to convey that the product being sold could improve everyday life by allowing the buyer to do routine tasks faster and better. As an added incentive, most Popeil products offered extra value by doing multiple tasks—all at a price anyone could afford. Viewers were also reminded that the product was a "great gift idea," and the company always secured maximum air time around important retail holidays, particularly Christmas, Mother's Day, and Father's Day.

The alchemy of the products and the commercials made Samuel and Raymond Popeil millionaires. Popeil Brothers became a successful publicly traded corporation in 1969. Samuel moved to a posh high-rise apartment overlooking Lake Michigan, which he shared with his second wife, Eloise, and their two daughters, Pamela and Lisa. He was driven each day to the Popeil factory in a chauffeur-driven Cadillac—a highly visible and satisfying symbol of his success.

The mid- to late 1970s was a period of difficulty for the company, though. In many ways, Popeil Brothers was a victim of its own success. In the company's early years, inexpensive television time was plentiful, but as time went on, it became scarcer and more expensive as other companies competed for choice time to air their commercials. Not only did other companies copy the Popeil Brothers' marketing techniques, but many of their former distributors started selling products of their own on television, including Samuel's son Ron. The company responded by dropping many of their longtime distributors, including Ron Popeil, and experimented with marketing their own products.

Another reason for the slowing momentum of Popeil Brothers' business in the late 1970s was the nature of the products themselves. As sophisticated electric appliances became more affordable, the appeal of the simple hand-operated Popeil gadgets gradually diminished.

By the late 1970s, Samuel Popeil's health had begun to decline, although he still continued to be active with his brother in the day-to-

ABOVE: **Ronco founders Ron Popeil and Mel Korey look every bit the part of successful young 1970s' businessmen when they posed for this publicity photograph (ca. 1972).**

day operations of the company. Rumors of impending changes at Popeil Brothers became a reality in September 1979, when the company was purchased by Milwaukee businessman Saul Padek. Rather than continue the business, he determined it was more profitable to dissolve the company. Within two years, the firm, its name, and its products had been liquidated.

Nonetheless, Samuel J. Popeil continued to dabble with new inventions until his death on July 15, 1984, at the age of sixty-nine. Four years later, on Christmas Day, 1988, Raymond Popeil died at sixty-seven. The brothers are buried at Chesed Shel Ames, the family cemetery located on a secluded hilltop overlooking Asbury Park, New Jersey. They were laid to rest with their parents and many members of the entrepreneurial Morris family.

In the true tradition of the "But, wait! There's more!" Popeil approach to life and business, this story of television pitchmanship has continued through Ron Popeil, who has taken television marketing to even greater heights and has become an internationally recognized celebrity in the process.

It is widely assumed that Ron Popeil and his firm, Ronco Teleproducts, was an outgrowth of his father and uncle's business, but they were separate entities. Because of his uneasy relationship with his father and uncle, Ron chose to start his own television marketing business in 1964 with his friend and former college roommate, Mel Korey. The firm started out small, with offices in the dining room of Ron's apartment. By 1973, Ronco Teleproducts, Inc. was a publicly traded corporation with net sales of over $20 million a year, with offices in the Playboy Building on Chicago's prestigious North Michigan Avenue.

A major difference between Popeil Brothers and Ronco was that Ron Popeil and Mel Korey chose not to manufacture their own products. By contracting with outside sources, they avoided the overhead and headaches associated with operating a factory. By this arrangement, Ronco was able to operate with only a small number of employees at its offices and warehouse, as opposed to the over three hundred people employed by his father and uncle at Popeil Brothers.

Ronco's inaugural television sales venture was a versatile plastic spray gun, simply called Spray Gun, that could be attached to an ordinary garden hose. By inserting special tablets into the nozzle, the spray gun could accomplish a number of cleaning and gardening chores—all for the price of $5.98. Low-budget commercials were made by a television station in Tampa, Florida, for $550. To save money, Ron used a friend's home and car for the shoot, and wrote the script and did the voice-over himself.

Once the commercial was filmed, Korey set out to buy commercial time from small television stations throughout the Midwest. At the same time, he convinced local merchants to carry the product offering them the incentive that their respective store's name would be mentioned at the end of the commercial. As a further incentive, Ronco agreed to take back any Spray Guns that did not sell. This method of guaranteed-sale merchandising was similar to the marketing technique used for years by Popeil Brothers and was repeated for most of Ronco's early promotions.

Ronco's first venture in telemarketing was an overwhelming success, as over one million Spray Guns were sold. Other early Ronco television promotions included Ron reselling Veg-O-Matics and Dial-O-Matics that he had purchased directly from his father's company, which in turn made his company one of Popeil Brothers' largest distributors. But Ron Popeil often rejected Popeil Brothers' ready-made commercials for those products and created his own to reflect his personal selling style.

A significant part of Ronco's sales in the late 1960s came from television promotions for London Aire hosiery, a brand of women's nylon stockings that were "guaranteed in writing" not to run. The product was introduced to Ron Popeil by a friend from England, hence the product's distinctive name, although the stockings themselves were manufactured in North Carolina. The commercial is a well-remembered classic, showing a pair of London Aires being subjected to repeated strokes of a nail file and a scouring pad, and being burned by a lit cigarette. As promised, they did not run.

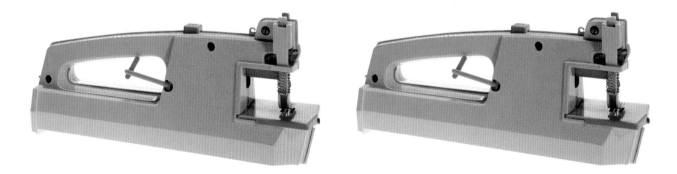

The identity of the Ronco Portable Sewing Machine as a product of the early 1970s comes through loud and clear in its distinctive colors and styling.

After several years of reselling commercially available products, Popeil and Korey introduced their first custom-manufactured household gadget in 1967, the Cordless Power Scissors. This was the first of a series of battery-powered (but always referred to as "cordless electric") small appliances that were made especially for Ronco by New England manufacturer Herman Brickman and New York–based product designer John S. Doyel. The earliest products were invented and manufactured entirely by Doyel and Brickman, but as time went on, Popeil became increasingly active in thinking up his own new items for production.

As an inventor and product developer, Popeil is truly his father's son. He often becomes consumed with each new Ronco product from its concept to its marketing, instinctually knowing what will work, and most importantly, what will sell. Like his father, he has also drawn on his years of experience as a pitchman to create seductive television commercials that convey their message with a firm, yet engaging hard-sell technique. The early Ronco commercials were essentially filmed demonstrations of the product at work, accompanied by Ron Popeil's carefully crafted script. Many Ronco commercials had less-than-perfect production quality, but their messages were most effective, for anyone seeing the colorfully packaged Ronco appliances at a store could not help but remember the product's television advertisement. As a reminder, each package was branded with the words "As Seen on TV," a slogan that is now ubiquitous.

Ronco occasionally used its television marketing expertise to pitch products for other companies. Dennison Manufacturing Company, a large producer of sewing goods, for example, initially had difficulty marketing a button-attaching tool called The Buttoneer until Ronco took over the promotion and sold millions of them. Similar success was achieved with Ronco's marketing of the Seal-A-Meal, a now-famous product that heat-sealed food into clear plastic pouches. Other well-known television items resold by Ronco included the Miracle Brush, a nappy reversible brush that was ideal for removing lint or pet hair from clothing or furniture, and the Hula Hoe, a garden tool that achieved television immortality as "the weeder with a wiggle."

Another secret of Ronco's success was keeping its products in sync with the times. During the 1970s, growing interest in handcrafts resulted in a number of related products, such as the Bottle and Jar Cutter, for recycling discarded glass bottles into decorative household accessories, and the Rhinestone and Stud Setter, for customizing clothing and accessories. Other such items included weaving looms, candle kits, and even a cordless electric pottery wheel with special clay that could be fired in an ordinary kitchen oven.

The 1970s also marked Ronco's entry into producing television-advertised record albums, most of which were anthologies of past pop music hits. The commercials typically featured breathless announcers promising "twenty original hits by the original artists!" as song excerpts blared in the background, and a seemingly endless scroll of song titles moved down the screen. Although not the first to produce records and commercials of this type, Ronco was one of the largest suppliers of television-advertised records in the 1970s and early 1980s; the company also launched a successful subsidiary in England. Never missing an opportunity to make an additional sale, the back of many record covers included advertisements for Ronco products, most notably the Ronco Record Vacuum.

Original Hits by the Original Artists

O ther successful Ronco products of the 1970s and early 1980s were television-advertised records offering "top hits by the original stars." Inspiration for entering the greatest hits records market came from K-Tel, one of Ronco's most formidable competitors in television marketing. Pop-music compilations like *Get It On*, *Good Vibrations*, and *Star Trackin' 76* featured brightly colored jackets, many of which have become classics of 1970s' graphic kitsch. The popularity of Ronco's record line led to the establishment of a branch in Great Britain that offered similar pop-music compilations, but more serious music selections, too. One example is the 1983 album of Handel's *The Messiah*, which revealed its Ronco origins by having the notorious "As Seen on TV" printed across its jacket.

By the mid-1970s, the well-publicized older Popeil and Ronco products had been around long enough that people had begun to look upon them with familiar, almost nostalgic feelings, despite the fact the commercials had often been regarded with irritation or contempt at the time they were aired. The introduction of offbeat products like the Inside-the-Shell Egg Scrambler garnered Ron Popeil numerous guest appearances on television talk and news shows, as well as frequent interviews in magazines and newspapers. Not only did people begin to recognize Ron Popeil's name and face as the originator of Ronco products, they also were beginning to think that he was the creator of his father's products as well.

A significant event in the evolution of the Popeil legend came about in 1976 when *Saturday Night Live* featured a parody of a classic pitch-style television advertisement. With a skit showing Dan Aykroyd promoting a fictional product called the Bass-O-Matic '76, in which he liquified a whole fish, the entire genre of pitch-style advertising began a journey towards becoming a part of popular culture legend.

The Bass-O-Matic routine triggered a new public awareness of Popeil and Ronco products. While most people had strong recollections of the television advertisements themselves, few ever thought about what made them different until they saw the classic elements satirized on shows like *Saturday Night Live*, or mentioned on late-night talk shows. Unlike most commercials that subtly seduced the viewer with cleverly crafted praises, music, and artistically composed imagery, the typical Popeil and Ronco promotion pulled no punches with a no-nonsense, in-your-face intensity that was hard to ignore— or forget. In fact, the modestly produced pitch-style Popeil and Ronco advertisements began to seem like archaic curiosities when compared to the increasingly slick production values of mainstream television commercials produced by major advertisers during the 1960s and 1970s. With increasing frequency the terms "Popeil," "Ronco," and "O-Matic" appeared in the popular print and broadcast media as a euphemism for gadget or items sold via television.

By the early 1980s, Ron Popeil began to upgrade his ever-increasing line of Ronco products. Recognizing that Popeil Brothers had encountered difficulties from the increasing competition from manufacturers of low-cost electric appliances, Ron Popeil and Mel Korey started to diversify Ronco's catalog with more sophisticated electric products. Ronco improved and updated its Food Dehydrator, which was marketed to the increasing number of people interested in eating natural, healthy food. Similarly, Ronco introduced the CleanAire Machine, a plug-in, electric room air cleaner that was intended to appeal to environmentally conscious consumers. Retailing for $30, the CleanAire Machine was a significant move away from the inexpensive gadgets of earlier years.

As Ronco worked to diversify its markets in the early 1980s, the firm enjoyed the benefit of a healthy credit line from the First National Bank of Chicago. When another major Chicago bank ran into serious financial difficulties due to defaulted loans, First National Bank began to take a closer look at its own loan portfolio. Although the bank had never experienced problems with Ronco, the size of the firm's outstanding debt prompted the bank to recall its loan in late 1983. As a result, Ronco was forced into bankruptcy in early 1984.

In the aftermath of the bankruptcy, Mel Korey moved to Scottsdale, Arizona, where he established an advertising agency. Ron Popeil remained in Chicago, where he tried to salvage the business by using his personal savings to buy back the remaining Ronco products and production tooling from the bankruptcy receivers. Not in a financial position to return to television, Popeil made a bold career choice. He packed up his products and sold them at county fairs and public events as he had done at the start of his career. Popeil's return to the fair circuit did much to replenish his financial resources and sharpen his demonstration skills. By 1987, the humbling task of hawking the surplus Ronco inventory was over, but the effort was worth it. From 1987 through 1990, Popeil considered himself to be in semiretirement, tinkering with new product ideas and working as a consultant to other companies.

In 1991, Popeil decided to return to television after making a deal to promote his Food Dehydrator on the home shopping program of USA Direct, a small satellite network owned by Fingerhut, the giant Minneapolis mail-order merchandiser. Fingerhut agreed to purchase twenty thousand Food Dehydrators provided Popeil himself would do the on-air promotions. Popeil's extended absence from television did not diminish his sales technique—the Ronco Food Dehydrator instantly became USA Direct's hottest-selling item.

Inspired by his success, Ron Popeil decided to make his own commercial for the Food Dehydrator. This was his first opportunity to create one of the distinctive twenty-eight-minute-and-thirty-second broadcasts that have come to be known as "infomercials," which were made possible by the deregulation of FCC time limits for television commercials during the 1980s. Ron Popeil knew that the extended length would give him ample time to weave an irresistible pitch.

Produced for $33,000, the new Ronco Food Dehydrator infomercial established the basic format of Popeil's subsequent promotions. The presentation was almost indistinguishable in appearance and format to an actual television talk show, complete with a hostess and a full studio audience. The stage was set up like a kitchen, with samples of the product being sold lining the counters. The star was Ron Popeil himself, who first briefly talked about some of his familiar past products as well as some of his father's classics like the Veg-O-Matic and Pocket Fisherman. This beginning segment played up Ron Popeil's established identity as a familiar figure of American popular culture and provided the perfect segue into his latest promotion.

Having completed his introduction, Popeil then made the product itself the star of the show. Popeil built his classic pitch as he seductively described and demonstrated the product's versatile features. As the pitch progressed, he would initiate interaction with the studio audience, sometimes taking testimonials from satisfied customers. Occasionally, the camera would cut to views of audience members reacting or nodding their heads in agreement—the television equivalent of live-demonstration pitchmen evoking reactions from the crowd.

In the true tradition of the pitchman's "turn," Popeil structured his infomercial to build in fervor until the price of the merchandise was finally revealed. He often used the classic "countdown" technique (see page 18) in which the "suggested retail" price is noted first, followed by a progressive lowering of the price. Because most of Ronco's 1990s' products were substantial appliances costing over $100, the final price was usually given in multiple payments, worded as "four easy payments of $39.95." The price was then followed up with the usual "But, wait! There's more!" offer of free accessories and recipes to sweeten the deal. One of Ron Popeil's unusual variations of the traditional turn was to announce that he would sell his products at a low price if the purchaser would "tell a friend" about it. He was fully aware that the purchasers were under no legal obligation to do this, yet a surprising number of buyers wrote him to say that they had fulfilled their part of the deal.

The success of the Ronco Food Dehydrator was soon followed by infomercials for products ranging from the Automatic Pasta Maker to the famous spray-on bald-spot masker, GLH Formula #9—often called "Hair in a Can." Ron Popeil's 1990s' counterpart to the fame of the Veg-O-Matic in the 1960s and Mr. Microphone in the 1970s was the Showtime Rotisserie, a countertop cooker introduced via infomercial in late 1998. Its familiar catch phrase in which Ron Popeil says, "Set it…" followed by the audience's chant, "…and forget it!" became one of the most familiar mantras of that decade's popular culture.

As Ron Popeil's career moved forward, he also reflected on the past. He rereleased some of the classic products made by his father and uncle at Popeil Brothers, including the stylish late-1950s' Dial-O-Matic, and the Pocket Fisherman. Popular older Ronco items like the Inside-the-Shell Egg Scrambler made a triumphant television comeback throughout the 1990s.

By the mid-1990s, Ron Popeil had firmly assumed the mantle as the high priest of unusual television-advertised inventions.

Through his years of hard work and public exposure, Ron Popeil has become a nationally recognized celebrity. In an appearance on the *CBS Evening News*, he was described as "a master, a pioneer, the king of the infomercial, a gadget savant." His name and products are routinely mentioned in all media, from movies to late-night talk shows. Songs have been written about him, and stories about his life and career have appeared in magazines from *People* to the *New Yorker*.

Today, Ron Popeil's business enterprises have become legendary not only in terms of popular culture fame, but also in business circles. With the Showtime Rotisserie having sold over three million units to date and the continuing steady sales of his other products, Popeil was estimated in 2001 by *Forbes* magazine to have an annual income of $20 million. In recent years, he has repeatedly stated that he is trying to sell his business so that he can devote his time exclusively to the creation of new inventions, but he has expressed no interest in retirement or slowing down. Ron Popeil's success unquestionably reflects his own hard work and perseverance, but at the same time, it echoes the presence of his father, his uncle, Raymond Popeil, and the generations of pitchmen that came before them.

They knew how to pitch magic.

Isn't that amazing?

The Popeil Brothers' earliest efforts were simple metal kitchen tools similar to everyday products made by other manu-facturers but often with a unique, creative twist that made them their own. Intended for sale to professional demonstrators and retail stores, these modest products were given attractive packaging that could

PUTTING THE PEDDLE TO THE METAL

draw attention in a pitchman's hand as well as sitting on a store shelf. In the true pitchman's tradition, the products were given catchy names and housed in colorful boxes. The offer of free recipes printed in booklets or directly on the box was also touted as an additional sales incentive.

Gadget-Master
M.S. TRADE MARK

SPIRAL SLICER

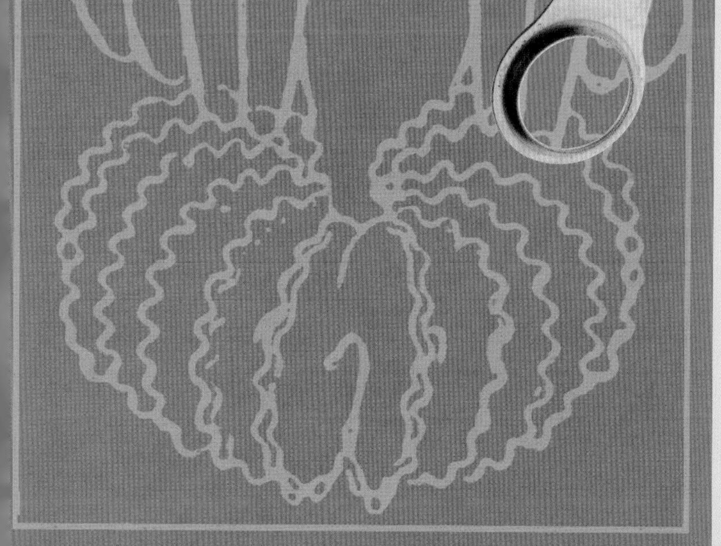

SPIRAL SLICER
(POPEIL BROTHERS/GADGET MASTER, 1946)

A cross between a knife and a corkscrew, the Spiral Slicer could hold crowds spellbound while a pitchman twirled it around a fruit or vegetable, transforming the food into a delicate springlike spiral. The product was the Popeil Brothers' own version of a classic pitchman's gadget.

FIG. No. 3

FIG. No. 4

PLATE AND PAN SCRAPER
(POPEIL BROTHERS/GADGET MASTER, 1946)

A decidedly low-tech item, this small product nevertheless included specific instructions on how to properly scrape a pan.

HOT VEGETABLE TONGS
(POPEIL BROTHERS/GADGET MASTER, 1946)

Spring-action tongs with forklike ends delivered an unfailing grip to everything from baked potatoes to canning jars.

AUTOMATIC EGG TURNER
(POPEIL BROTHERS/GADGET MASTER, 1948)

Popeil Brothers often brought an element of surprise to the ordinary. With just a slight squeeze of the spring-wire handle, the blade of this seemingly ordinary spatula would rotate just enough to perfectly turn an egg or a pancake.

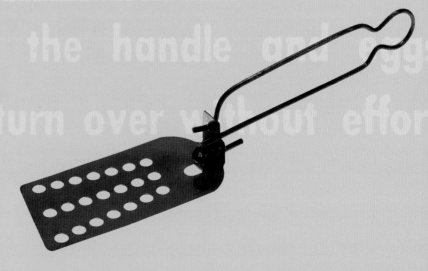

Handy for serving fried chicken or piping hot corn-on-the-cob

Helpful in turning steaks or roasts

Indispensable for removing fruit jars from boiling water

GRATER SHREDDER
(POPEIL BROTHERS/GADGET MASTER, 1948)

The paddlelike design and single-hand grip of this grater made it easier to hold and control than other graters, thus diminishing the chances of scraping a knuckle or finger.

TOASTY PIE
(POPEIL BROTHERS, 1950)

Popeil Brothers was one of many companies to make versions of this device that made toasted pocket sandwiches.

U.S. PATENT APPLIED FOR DESIGN

POPEIL'S
TOASTY-PIE

TASTY SANDWICH-PIES

TURNS 2 SLICES OF BREAD AND YOUR FAVORITE FILLING INTO A PIE OR HOT SEALED TOASTED SANDWICH

RECIPES & DIRECT

Attractive yet practical, Popeil Brothers' plastic kitchenware from the late 1940s and early 1950s represented the firm's classic period of product design. With elegant, minimalist modernity, these products demonstrated the potential of plastics from an artistic and business standpoint.

Bold colors, textures, and shapes transformed everyday kitchen tools into attractive objects suitable for

CLASSIC PLASTICS

decorative display, instead of relegation to cupboards and drawers. Plastics also had the advantage of being rustproof, with smooth, seamless shapes that were easy to clean. The same clean-lined simplicity also made the products efficient to manufacture and lightweight to transport. As a result, costs were substantially reduced for the manufacturer, distributor, and consumer.

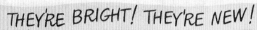

THEY'RE BRIGHT! THEY'RE NEW!

MADE OF STYRON

MEASURE FOR MEASURE, these bright Styron measuring cups are smart kitchen aids. By Quinn-Berry Corporation, 2601 W. 12th St., Erie, Pa., for Hutzler Manufacturing Company, 4821 Skillman Ave., Long Island City, N.Y.

SERVE IT OR SAVE IT in this smooth, modern eight-inch Styron dish, smartly designed for table or storage. It's as useful as it is good looking. By F & F Mold & Die Works, 103 Sachs Street, Dayton 3, Ohio.

COOKIES ARE MORE FUN when this gay, new Styron Cooky Press does the shaping. By Makray Mfg. Co., 1419 Diversey Pkwy., Chicago, Illinois, for Popeil Brothers, 556 West Congress St., Chicago, Illinois.

NINE LIVES are in store for this smart, handy Styron 4½" utility bowl. It's efficient and decorative for serving or storage. By The Burroughs Company, 3831 Verdugo Road, Los Angeles 41, California.

KEEP IT FRESH in this clever, molded-of-Styron refrigerator dish with a crystal clear top. Rounded corners make it easy to clean, too! By Claremould Plastics Company, 200 Wright St., Newark 5, N.J.

These Styron products are sold at leading department stores.

Plastics manufacturers placed advertisements like this one in popular magazines such as the *Saturday Evening Post* to overcome public skepticism about plastic products. One of the items shown was Popeil Brothers' Cooky Press.

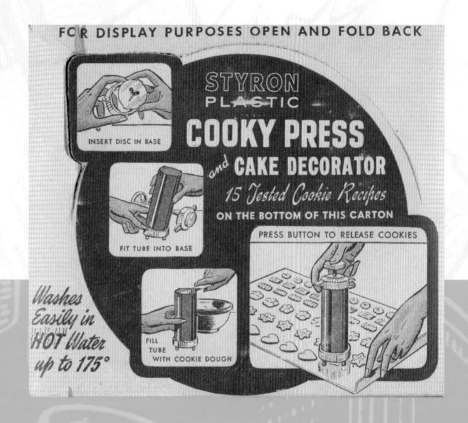

FOR DISPLAY PURPOSES OPEN AND FOLD BACK

INSERT DISC IN BASE

STYRON PLASTIC

COOKY PRESS *and* **CAKE DECORATOR**

15 Tested Cookie Recipes
ON THE BOTTOM OF THIS CARTON

FIT TUBE INTO BASE

PRESS BUTTON TO RELEASE COOKIES

Washes Easily in **HOT Water** *up to 175°*

FILL TUBE WITH COOKIE DOUGH

COOKY PRESS
(POPEIL BROTHERS/
GADGET MASTER, 1948)

Popeil Brothers' first plastic product was a colorful version of the traditional metal cookie press.

FLOUR SIFTER
(POPEIL BROTHERS, 1950)

Considerably more attractive than old-fashioned metal sifters, Popeil Brothers' plastic version was pitched as having "trigger action" that could "sift faster and finer."

DONUT MAKER
(POPEIL BROTHERS, 1950)

For $1, the Popeil Donut Maker merged beauty and utility with its gracefully tapering shape that allowed the doughnut batter to flow unimpeded to the bottom. By depressing the red wooden knob at the top, a plunger released perfect rings of dough into the frying pan. Attractive color contrasts were achieved by using two different types of plastic for its component parts. This device was remarketed in the early 1960s as the Minit Chef Automatic Pancaker.

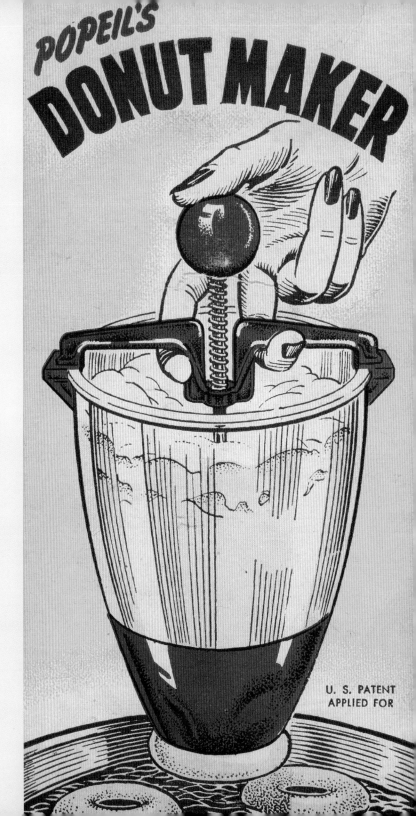

POPEIL'S DONUT MAKER

U. S. PATENT APPLIED FOR

minit chef *

AUTOMATIC

PANCAKER*

HOLDS 18 FOUR INCH PANCAKES

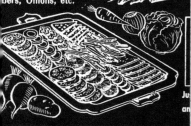

SLICE-A-WAY
(POPEIL BROTHERS, 1950)

Barely over three inches high and six inches long, this strikingly animated plastic platform cutter appears to boldly kick up its backside to provide the ideal angle for efficient slicing. Ron Popeil refused to demonstrate the Slice-a-Way because it lacked a blade guard. He claimed that "if you slipped, it could slice you up to the elbow."

A classic pitchman's item, the Citrex Juicer gave oranges and lemons their own built-in pouring spout. The Citrex was often a bonus giveaway distributed in conjunction with another product.

WORLD'S SMALLEST FRUIT JUICE EXTRACTOR

Extracts the Juice from 6 Oranges in less than 3 Minutes.

No. 162—Cake Cover
Size: 12" Diam., 7" High.

BREADBOX
(POPEIL BROTHERS, 1952)

The timeless simplicity of Popeil Brothers' plastic breadbox is betrayed only by the stylized 1950s' lettering used on the cover.

141—3-Pc. Canister Set
64 oz.

NEW HAND PAINTED LINE
OF *Plastic Kitchenware*

Each piece beautifully decorated with the popular
Tea Rose design— America's favorite decorative motif!

by POPEIL

STACKING CANISTERS
(POPEIL BROTHERS, 1952)

These simple cylinders of marbleized and opaque plastic could either be lined up or stacked on a counter or shelf to conserve space in small kitchens.

No. 328—"Trigger Action"
2-cup Flour Sifter.

HAND-PAINTED CANISTERS
(POPEIL BROTHERS, 1952)

By hand-painting floral patterns on plastic kitchenware, Popeil Brothers offered a modern alternative to the hand-decorated metal products made by other manufacturers. The practice of hand-painting kitchenware goes back centuries to the floral designs commonly painted on sheet metal or tin plate known as toleware.

GRATE 'N SHRED
(POPEIL BROTHERS, 1951)

It was almost impossible to hurt your hands on the gentle plastic surfaces of the Grate 'n Shred—a vast improvement over the Popeil Brothers' 1948 metal knuckle-buster version on page 38.

The public readily associates the "O-Matic" suffix with everything Popeil, but the truth is, the Popeils were not the first to use it. Derived from the word "automatic," the term had been used decades before to create the illusion of ease and efficiency for everything from flatirons to fountain pens.

Even if Popeil Brothers didn't originate

MEET THE O-MATICS

the term "O-Matic," their television commercials and products made it indelibly their own. "O-Matic" had the perfect sound and look for their television-advertised products and has entered the American popular culture lexicon as a universally used suffix to convey gadget-related imagery.

C H O P · O · M A T I C   C O M M E R C I A L   (1 9 5 6)

Ladies and gentlemen, I'm going to show you the greatest kitchen appliance ever made—it's called

Chop-O-Matic. The secret of this remarkable machine is every time I tap on the knob, the blades rotate

automatically. That's what makes Chop-O-Matic so amazing. The next time that you bake a cake, or if

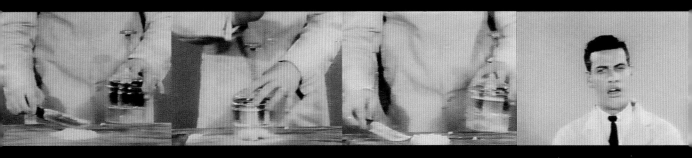

you're going to make some homemade candies, or serve some of those delicious ice cream sundaes,

add all the chopped walnuts, pecans, cashews, and almonds you wish. It takes only seconds to add

that fine richness and flavor to all your desserts. For chopping celery, place your celery under the

container—a few taps—your chopping chores are over and your celery is finely chopped. For those

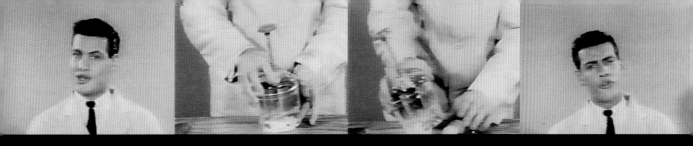

delicious potato pancakes, place your potatoes under the machine—a few taps—a few seconds—those potato pancakes won't fall apart, and they won't be tasteless or rubbery as when you grate them. And just look how fine these potatoes are! Now folks, I'll show you the crowning feature of this marvelous new machine. For now, you can chop three or four whole onions at one time. Here's where your

Chop-O-Matic will save the day for both your hands and your eyes. You chop those onions so fine, all your onions are chopped to perfection without shedding a single tear. For that delicious California health salad, we're going to use some radishes, we'll use some green pepper, and some carrots, too. We'll place some celery under the machine also. Now I'm going to place all these vegetables under the

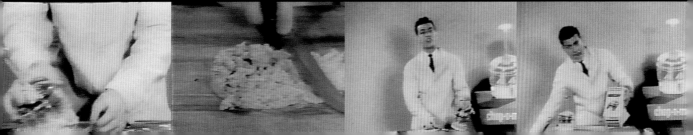

machine at one time—a few taps—and down and around those six stainless steel chopping blades go, always safe and sure. Pour some salad dressing over the top, and it not only looks appetizing, but it's equally delicious. Everyone likes cole slaw—everyone, that is, except Mother. The reason she doesn't like it is because she's the one who's got to make it on that old grater—and oh, the scrapes on her poor knuckles. Well, here's where your Chop-O-Matic comes to the rescue. Place that cabbage under the container and start tapping. You know, why, even the youngsters will be glad to help if you'll let them. And just look how fine this cole slaw is made! Why, you'll never get indigestion eating cole slaw made this way. But you men will love it just for crushing ice. Place those ice cubes under the blades and chop away. Crushed ice is ideal for mixed drinks, for chilled seafoods and desserts. And for those snow cones for the youngsters, why, it will be a real treat. For that egg salad, why, you can put four full eggs under the machine at one time. Let me show you how fine and quickly you can make that egg salad. A few taps and in practically no time you have that egg salad made just the way you want it. I know you're all wondering what this machine sells for. Well, Chop-O-Matic will be nationally advertised for $5.98, and it's well worth it. During this special television presentation, if you order right now, the price is not $5.98, but only three dollars and ninety-eight cents—that's right—just three dollars and ninety-eight cents! And, ladies and gentlemen, if you just use this machine for chopping your prepared meats alone, why, it'll be worth twice that much to you. You know, ham for ham salad, chicken for chicken salad, corned beef for corned beef hash. For roast beef too and for those chopped livers—why, it's wonderful! You chop that meat so fine, you make it into a sandwich spread as I've done here. To clean the machine, you just rinse it in warm soapy water. The blades are rustproof—they're stainless steel. And as a special bonus, during this television offer, you will receive with your Chop-O-Matic, at no additional charge, a valuable recipe book containing fifty secret recipes by world-famous chefs. Now here's your announcer to tell you how to order.

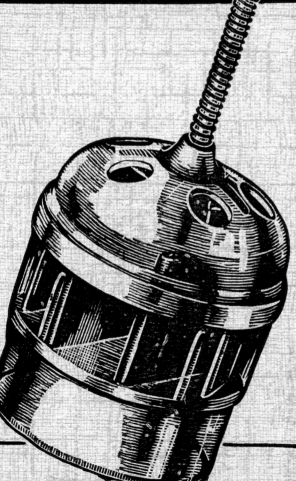

chop·o·matic

New... just tap it!

FOOD CHOPPER

Automatic rotating
stainless steel blades

CHOP-O-MATIC
(POPEIL BROTHERS, 1956)

The first Popeil Brothers product to bear the
"O-Matic" name was the 1956 Chop-O-Matic,
a clear plastic-domed chopper that simultaneously chopped and mixed food. It also has the
honor of being the first product pitched by
Ron Popeil on television. The product was
plagued by patent infringement litigation that
resulted in its simplification and redesign in
the early 1960s.

chop·o·matic's

fabulous new mate

DELUXE
Dial-O-Matic*
FOOD CUTTER

performs miracles with food!

DIAL-O-MATIC
(POPEIL BROTHERS, 1958)

Introduced as the "Chop-O-Matic's fabulous new mate," the Dial-O-Matic could slice foods in varied thicknesses with the simple turn of a dial. It also featured a blade guard to keep fingers away from the cutting blade—a vast improvement over the unprotected blade of the earlier Slice-a-Way. The Dial-O-Matic was flashy. It was two-toned and styled with an upward rear thrust reminiscent of the tail fins of a 1958-era car. To keep the product up-to-date, the Dial-O-Matic's 1950s' styling was replaced in 1976 with a space-age design called the Dial-O-Matic Mark Four. In the 1990s, Ron Popeil reintroduced the 1958 version of the device in all its retro glory.

New, fabulous Dial-O-Matic makes you a master chef in minutes! Now, you can perform miracles with food with no more effort than a flick of your wrist!

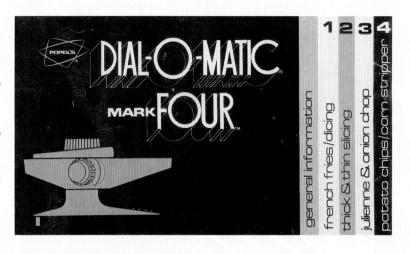

Dial-O-Matic does the work for you. Shreds cabbage ... makes julienne (or shoestring) potatoes, beets, carrots, cheese straws ... turns out waffle potatoes and beets ... cuts corn from the cob ... wonderful for ripple potatoes ... slices citrus fruits, apples, bananas, eggplant, onions, tomatoes, cucumbers, carrots, celery, radishes, olives, etc. Dial-O-Matic

also helps you prepare glamorous garnishes that will add eye and appetite appeal to everything from banquet dinners to the simplest family meals!

–Dial-O-Matic instruction book, 1959

Mention the Veg-O-Matic to almost anyone, and he or she will usually respond by chanting "It slices! It dices!" Although most people swear that these words were actually spoken in the Veg-O-Matic commercials, the sobering truth is that they were not. Ron Popeil compares this phenomenon to famous, yet unspoken movie lines, like Cary Grant's alleged "Judy, Judy, Judy," and Humphrey Bogart's often mis-quoted *Casablanca* line "Play it again, Sam."

The phrase "It slices! It dices!" may have been fictitious, but the Veg-O-Matic's success was real, as a result of the television advertisements that made it famous and Popeil Brothers' most successful product.

Samuel J. Popeil's product concept was shaped by the Chicago design studio of Edward Klein, who gave its high-impact plastic frame classic 1960s' styling that included a chevronlike "V" insignia— a symbol that could be found on everything from contemporary cigarette packs to painted designs on suburban garage doors. Veg-O-Matic's television campaign was first launched in 1961, but was soon withdrawn due to customer complaints about the blades breaking. Improved and reintroduced in 1963, the Veg-O-Matic enjoyed legendary success.

The Veg-O-Matic continued to be the mainstay of the Popeil Brothers line for over fifteen years and held a featured place in the company catalog as long as Samuel and Raymond Popeil ran the company. Throughout the Veg-O-Matic's many years in production, its creators were confident that they were providing the public with a quality product that would provide years of useful service. Evidence of this attitude can be found in a small flyer that was included with each

There's Never Been Anything Like It!

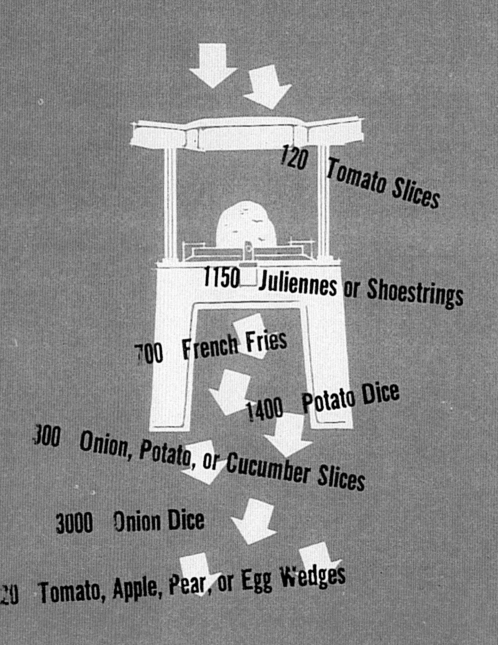

Veg-O-Matic and listed spare parts that could be ordered to keep the slicer in prime operating condition. Rather than sell the consumer an entirely new machine for $7.77, Popeil Brothers was happy to send out replacement parts, some costing as little as twenty-five cents.

As demonstrated on the commercial, the Veg-O-Matic could rapidly slice or dice a wide variety of foods, but its integrity was challenged in 1971, when an attorney tried to slice a tomato as shown on the commercial, but burst it all over his kitchen instead. Not content to clean up the mess and forget it, he filed a well-publicized fraudulent advertising complaint with the Federal Trade Commission. Samuel J. Popeil defended his brainchild like a proud father, pointing out that the procedures outlined in the instructions had not been followed. Even Ron Popeil came to the defense of his father's invention, stating to a reporter for *The Chicagoan* magazine in 1973: "As for the FTC's charges against my father and the Veg-O-Matic, my answer is, I have a

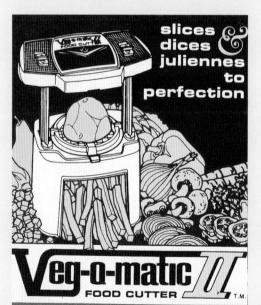

piano at home but I don't know how to play it. Does that mean it doesn't work?"

Popeil Brothers ultimately prevailed in the suit, but the Veg-O-Matic was subsequently modified and supplied with new directions to make it more tomato-friendly. By the mid-1970s, sales began to slip as the Veg-O-Matic began to compete with sophisticated low-priced electric appliances that were entering the market. In an attempt to create an updated image, the Popeils reintroduced the machine as the Veg-O-Matic II in 1975, although the only major change was the cosmetic replacement of the 1960s-style label on the plunger with a new 1970s-style version in simulated wood grain. After the dissolution of Popeil Brothers, the Veg-O-Matic was reintroduced by former Popeil distributor and later competitor K-Tel, and is still available today.

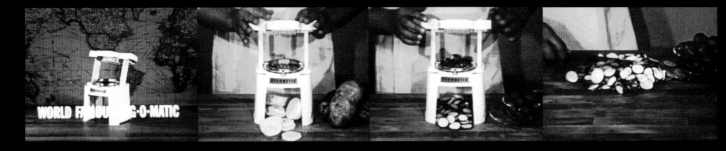

T H E   V E G - O - M A T I C   C O M M E R C I A L

(C I R C A   1 9 6 5)

Here's the world-famous Veg-O-Matic that slices whole potatoes completely with one motion. Or bunches of radishes in

seconds! Imagine slicing a whole firm tomato with one stroke. Hamburger lovers, like magic, whole onions become tempt-

ing thin slices. Simply turn the dial and thick-slice an entire can of prepared meat at once. Isn't that amazing!?!! Dial from

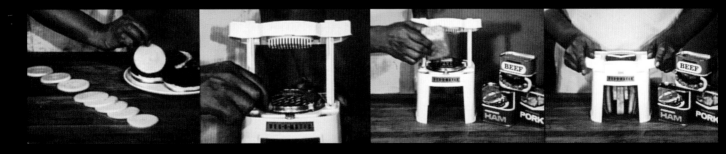

slice to dice. Veg-O-Matic makes mounds of diced onions—fast—without tears! For everybody's

favorite, French fries—hundreds of them in just one minute! Over a million Veg-O-Matics sold at

$9.95. Here's your chance to own one for only $7.77. And at no extra cost, we'll include this excit-

ing booklet. Save money by ordering Veg-O-Matic now while it's available at only $7.77.

CORN-O-MATIC
(FEATURE PRODUCTS/POPEIL BROTHERS, 1964)

Often given away as a "But, wait! There's more!" bonus product, this corn-shaped device efficiently stripped corn from the cob and also performed extra duty as a corer and cookie cutter.

Stuffed Dill Pickle—Cut pickle in half—insert serrated cutter over soft core. Twist gently, at same time pressing forward. When cutter is completely embedded, insert a knife through back end of cutter and twist to remove soft core. Stuff with cream cheese—serve sliced.

MINCE-O-MATIC SEVEN
(FEATURE PRODUCTS/POPEIL BROTHERS, 1965)

The Mince-O-Matic Seven was a versatile, hand-cranked food processor with a numerical name that proved to be more than just promotional flair. A mincer, chopper, grater, ricer, blender, juicer, and food mill, it was seven appliances in one! Samuel Popeil was especially proud of its powerful suction grip that held it firmly to a counter or table.

mince O matic *Seven*

·MINCER·CHOPPER·GRATER·RICER·BLENDER·JUICER·FOOD M

·MINCER·CHOPPER·GRATER·RICER·BLENDER·JUICER·FOOD M

Scallop
form
corer over grape. Lift core and twist back and forth, pressing lightly. When corer touches bottom, pry slightly, core will lift out.

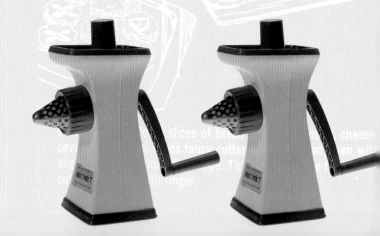

PEEL◉MATIC*
TOMATO PEELER

ALSO PEELS
ONIONS
PEACHES
PEARS
PLUMS

DIRECTIONS

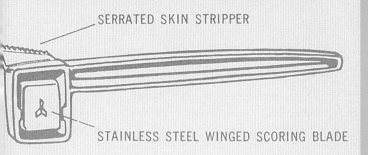

SERRATED SKIN STRIPPER

STAINLESS STEEL WINGED SCORING BLADE

PEEL-O-MATIC
(FEATURE PRODUCTS/POPEIL BROTHERS, 1965)

Another product used as a giveaway with the purchase of a larger item, the Peel-O-Matic did exactly what its name implies—it scored the skin of fruits and vegetables for easy peeling.

Whip-O Wallbanger

1 oz. vodka
½ oz. galliano
1 teaspoon cream
10 oz. (approximately) orange juice
Whip well with shaved ice in your Whip-O-Matic. Strain into 12 oz. frosted collins glass. Garnish with citrus fruit.

WHIP-O-MATIC (POPEIL BROTHERS, 1974)

The last product to bear the O-Matic name, the Whip-O-Matic was also distinguished as one of Popeil Brothers' most technically sophisticated products. This hand-cranked device could whip any liquid into a frothy, aerated mixture—perfect for eggs, pancakes, mixed drinks, whipped cream, or meringues. Its three orbiting mixing paddles were touted as having "planetary action."

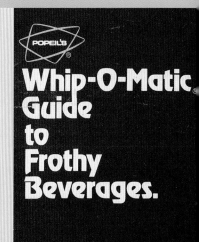

POPEIL'S®
Whip-O-Matic®
Guide to Frothy Beverages.

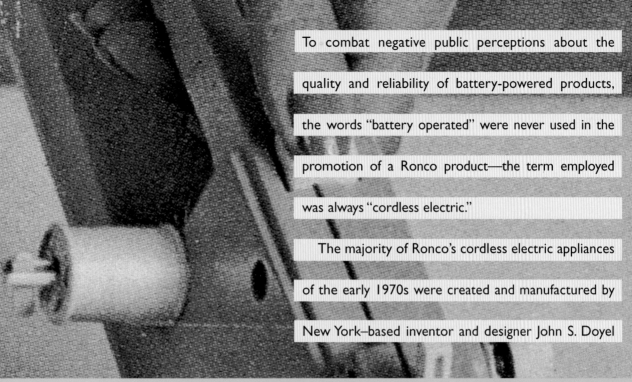

To combat negative public perceptions about the quality and reliability of battery-powered products, the words "battery operated" were never used in the promotion of a Ronco product—the term employed was always "cordless electric."

The majority of Ronco's cordless electric appliances of the early 1970s were created and manufactured by New York–based inventor and designer John S. Doyel

NEVER SAY BATTERY OPERATED—IT'S CORDLESS ELECTRIC!

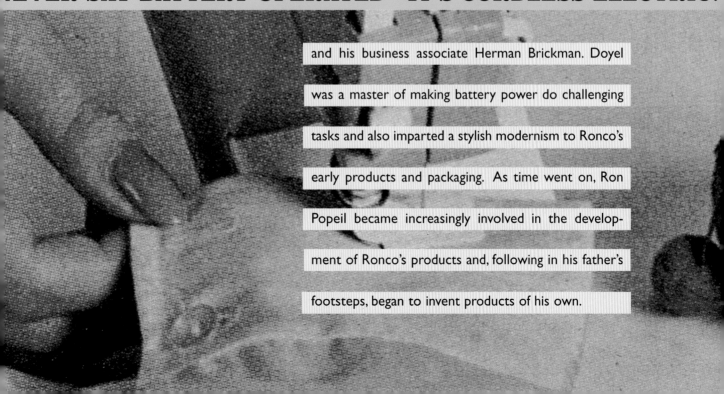

and his business associate Herman Brickman. Doyel was a master of making battery power do challenging tasks and also imparted a stylish modernism to Ronco's early products and packaging. As time went on, Ron Popeil became increasingly involved in the development of Ronco's products and, following in his father's footsteps, began to invent products of his own.

CORDLESS POWER SCISSORS
(RONCO MANUFACTURING CORPORATION, 1967)

This battery-operated scissors for sewing and crafts was Ronco's first television-advertised gadget. Advertised as the "scissors with the hole in the handle," it was originally created by John S. Doyel and Herman Brickman for another company, but was acquired as an exclusive Ronco product after the original client defaulted on its order.

GARDEN TRIMMER
(RONCO MANUFACTURING COMPANY, 1970) →

Looking like a spaceship out of *Star Trek*, the cordless electric Garden Trimmer was a useful portable lawn and garden tool that predated the proliferation of commercially available portable trimmers. Ronco and Popeil Brothers often updated their commercials and packaging to keep up with modern tastes and trends, as evidenced by the Garden Trimmer's restrained early 1970s' box and its psychedelic counterpart from later in the decade. Despite its safeguards, consumer injuries gave this product a short existence in the Ronco television catalog.

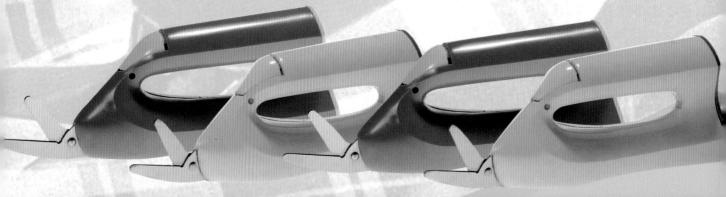

'Ronco' CORDLESS ELECTRIC

GARDEN TRIMMER

AS SEEN ON TV

Ronco

Garden Trimmer

BATTERIES NOT INCLUDED

handy product could even hem a dress while still wearing it. The product's styling and color is classic 1970s' Ronco chic.

AS SEEN ON TV

Ronco™

cordless electric
PORTABLE SEWING MACHINE

MIRACLE BROOM
(RONCO TELEPRODUCTS, 1973)

The package illustration for this portable vacuum portrays an image that modern families of the 1970s could relate to—cigarette butts being whisked out of bright green shag carpeting. While perhaps not exactly what could be called a miracle, this small portable vacuum was the forefather of later products like the Dust Buster. Cordless electric, it could be

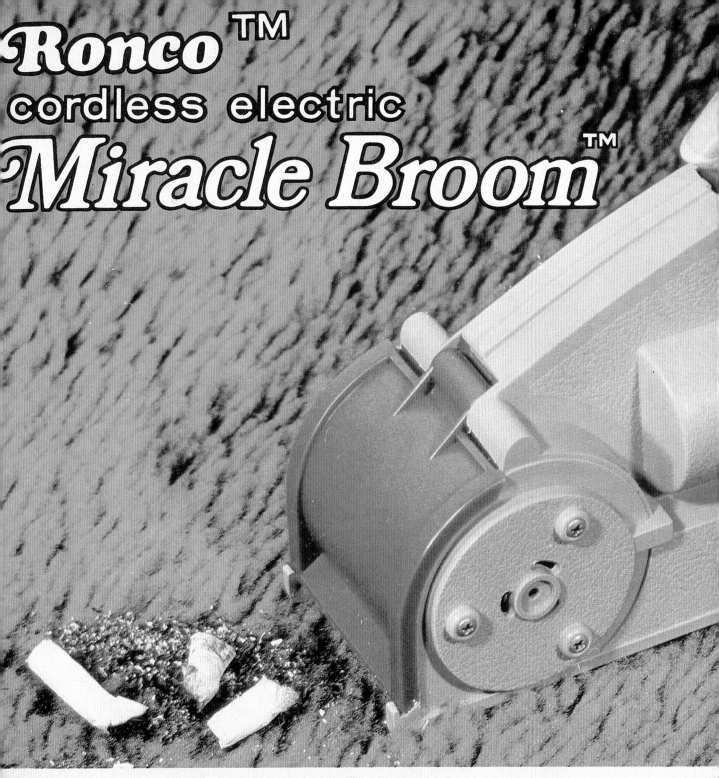

Ronco ™
cordless electric
Miracle Broom ™

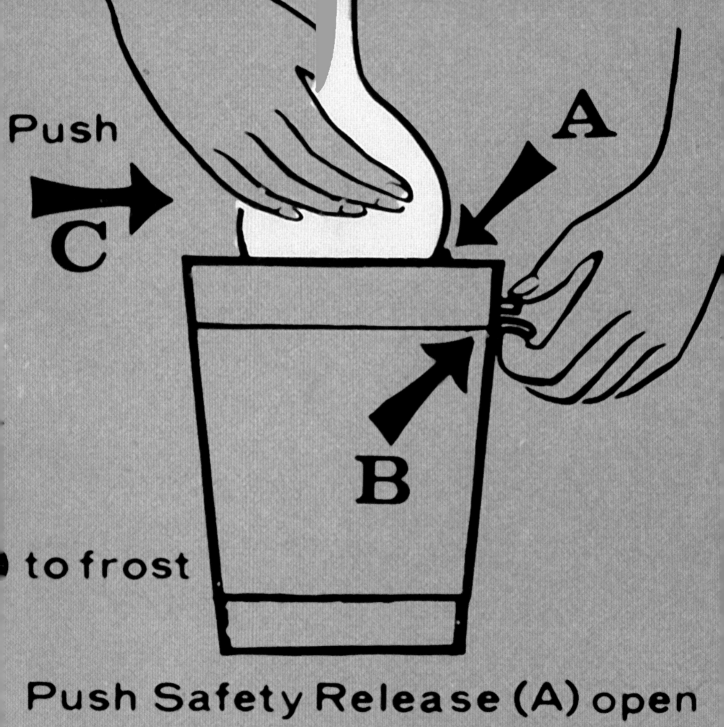

Push

C

A

B

to frost

Push Safety Release (A) open
with bottom edge of glass, in
direction of arrow (C)

Some inventions seem so simple and logical, they inspire people to wonder why they didn't think of the concept themselves. But many Popeil and Ronco products were so offbeat, they often inspired people to wonder *who* on earth could come up with them and, further, ponder why they would *ever* need them. Nevertheless, the commercials often turned

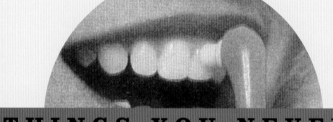

THINGS YOU NEVER KNEW YOU NEEDED

skeptics into converts. In fact, people not only bought the product for themselves, but also took the Popeils' suggestion that what they were buying was a "great gift idea." And even if people somehow decided that they could actually live *without* the product, the reassuring promise of a money-back guarantee often cinched the deal.

Ron Popeil wishes he had invented . . .
"the Clapper, because it was so simple,"
He confided to a Chicago Tribune reporter
in 1999 about the well-known TV
gadget that turns electrical appliances on
and off with the clap of a hand.
"I got mad at myself for not thinking of it."

SPRAY GUN
(RONCO, 1964)

Ronco's first television-promoted product was a plastic spray attachment that could make an ordinary garden hose perform a range of tasks, from washing and waxing a car to fertilizing a lawn. The sales of over a million Spray Guns successfully launched Ron Popeil and Mel Korey's telemarketing careers.

THE OLD WAY   THE RONCO WAY

Ronco ™

Outside inside

MAGNETIC

WINDOW WASHER

Pat. No. 3,296,645

Cleans the INSIDE and the OUTSIDE at the SAME TIME!

Ronco

OUTSIDE INSIDE

INSIDE-OUTSIDE WINDOW WASHER
(RONCO, INC., 1972)

These powerful magnetic pads cleaned hard-to-reach outside windows automatically while you safely cleaned the inside! The two magnetic cleaning pads were placed on each side of the glass. As you rubbed the inside cleaning pad, the outside pad cleaned in magnetic unison. In a test conducted on the windows at Ronco's eighteenth-story office in downtown Chicago, the outside unit lost magnetic contact and plunged to the busy street below. A safety string was subsequently added to prevent similar mishaps.

ICE CREAM MACHINE
(RONCO TELEPRODUCTS, 1974)

Everyone loves homemade ice cream, but nobody likes dealing with the messy ice and salt required for conventional ice cream freezers. With the Ronco Ice Cream Machine, all you had to do was pour your favorite ice cream recipe directly into the tub and place the whole unit in your freezer. Cordless electric power paddled the mixture into delicious ice cream in just twenty minutes!

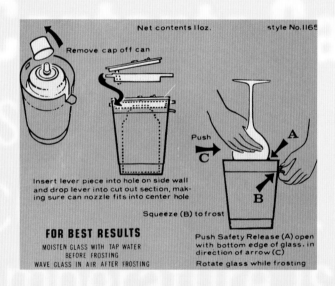

GLASS FROSTER
(RONCO TELEPRODUCTS, 1975)

Giving glassware a frosty glaze with the Ronco Glass Froster was not without its dangers. Although not a widely-held concern at the time of its release, a dose of atmosphere-eating gas was shot into the environment every time the device frosted a glass. Sternly worded notices on the box also warned that inhaling or misusing the contents could be fatal.

RECORD=VACUUM
cordless
electric

by **Ronco**™

ASPiRATEUR POUR DiSQUES
sans cordon
électrique

de **Ronco**™

Comme à la TV

As seen on TV

RECORD VACUUM
(RONCO TELEPRODUCTS, 1976)

In the pre-CD era, a few spins in the Ronco Record Vacuum could have record albums looking and sounding like new. With this device, dirt, dust, and static electricity could no longer diminish the enjoyment of your record collection. Bilingual packaging reminded French-Canadian shoppers that this was the same product that was "comme a la TV."

Ronco Auto Cup for Skiing

AUTO CUP
(RONCO TELEPRODUCTS, 1977)

Spillproof cups for automobiles are now commonplace, but the Auto Cup was an innovative concept when it was introduced. Ronco designer John S. Doyel created this insulated plastic cup with a spring-activated plug to prevent spillage.

HOLD-UP
(RONCO TELEPRODUCTS, 1978)

Ron Popeil considers Hold-Up to be one of his product disappointments, yet it's a good example of how an invention can come close, but not close enough, to a good idea. The Hold-Up was essentially a foam bulletin board coated with a weak adhesive that could be used to affix papers and notes without tacks. It was introduced two years before its technological opposite—Post-it™ Notes—was sold.

POPEIL'S SIT-ON™

TRASH COMPACTOR

TRASH BAGS

Heavy Duty
Compactor Quality

STOCK NO. CB-8

8 BAGS & TIES
9 IN. X 8 IN. X 28½ IN.

SIT-ON TRASH COMPACTOR
(POPEIL BROTHERS, 1978)

Even S.J. Popeil used to laugh about this bizarre garbage compactor that did its job by having someone sit on a plunger affixed to its lid. During the search for an appropriate name for this product, Popeil patent attorney Jack Dominik made an unheeded suggestion to call it the "Ash Basher." For all its strangeness, it still saved space in landfills by crushing trash without electricity or other environment-depleting resources. You didn't need to be physically fit to use it—the heavier you were, the better it worked.

MR. MICROPHO

Micro sans fi
en toute liber

**Fun and usef
for all ages**

Cordless, Wireless
Microphone
No
Attaching
Wires

your
ce on
radio!

Faites-vous
entendre
en FM!

Jtile et agréable
pour tous

Just as Samuel and Raymond Popeil's Veg-O-Matic was the television-advertised pop culture icon of the 1960s, prodigal son Ron Popeil's Mr. Microphone was the pop-culture symbol of the 1970s. A novelty item with no real purpose except for having fun, Mr. Microphone was a wireless transmitter that could broadcast up to a hundred feet away into any FM radio tuned to the proper frequency. Ron Popeil got the idea for the product after seeing a professional wireless microphone being used on the set of a television studio.

The television commercial was a major factor in Mr. Microphone's pop-culture immortality, showing a teenage boy in a car using Mr. Microphone to contact a radio-toting girl on the street with the now-famous pick-up line: "Hey, good lookin', I'll be back to pick you up later!" Familiar references to Mr. Microphone turn up virtually every-where, from the popular animated television series *The Simpsons* to its appearance in the Walt Disney film *Toy Story*.

Thanks to Mr. Microphone, the prefix "Mr." has joined Popeil Brothers' "O-Matic" as an appendage often jokingly applied to gadgetlike products and inventions. Promoted on television for $14.88, the wildfire popularity of Mr. Microphone led to numerous knock-offs by other companies, which ultimately led to the demise of the original in the early 1980s.

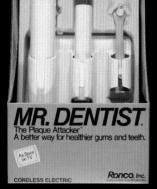

Despite what its name suggests, Mr. Dentist is *not* a cordless electric drill for home dentistry but a cordless electric home version of the rubber-tipped tool used by dentists to clean teeth.

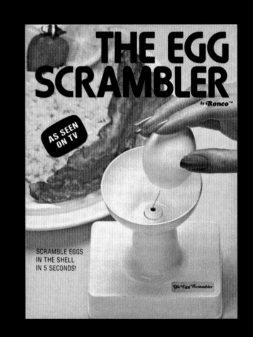

INSIDE-THE-SHELL EGG SCRAMBLER
(RONCO TELEPRODUCTS, 1978)

Yes—this product actually scrambles an egg while it is still inside its shell and was inspired by Ron Popeil's dislike of egg whites in his scrambled eggs. The Scrambler looks like an oversized eggcup with a bent pin sticking up from the bottom. When a fresh egg is carefully impaled on the needle, the downward pressure activates a button, causing the needle to rapidly rotate inside the egg. Perfectly blended scrambled eggs can be effortlessly cracked into the frying pan without the inconvenience of washing a mixing bowl or fork. Admirers of this device include homemaking guru Martha Stewart, who finds that it makes a perfect one-egg crepe.

In five minutes, I can sell anything. Five

minutes for me is a chance to mine gold.

—Ron Popeil, 1987

BOB

s and ringlets give
a youthful, bobbed
eamset rollers and set
ck hair vertically as
n bangs in place first.
e vertical rollers care-
ringlets by brushing
curl around finger.
ets at sides and tie
s. Brush neck curls

Classic
Hair Setting Patterns
and Styles

with **Steamset**
PERSONAL HAIRDRESSER

THE RINGLET RUFF

Crescent bangs and a halo of
ringlets. Set on Steamset rollers.
Remove top rollers first, brushing
out crown and bangs. Take down
remaining rollers one at a time.
Divide each curl into three sec-
tions. Comb each section individually around finger, spray and
hold briefly. Arrange all curls in
place before spraying entire hair
style.

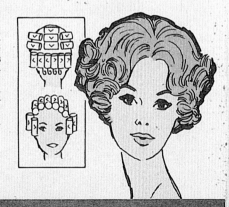

O RUFF

with a part. Set on
lers. Note that one
rtical. Use clip curls
move curlers care-
vertical curls intact.
ray from part, back-
nooth. Individually
curls around finger.
es and ringlets for-

THE VERY CURLY-DO

These curls, brushed to a gleam-
ing smoothness, are set on
Steamset rollers as shown.
Remove rollers carefully. Brush
each curl separately over a finger.
If hair lacks sufficient body,
spray while brushing. Arrange
curls around face and crown

Steamset
PERSONAL HAIRDRESSER

As television shows increasingly brought the latest styles and fashions into American homes, Popeil Brothers and Ronco both sought to diversify their wares into areas relating to health, beauty, and grooming. After years of promoting hand-operated kitchen gadgets, Popeil Brothers introduced their electric Steamset women's hair-roller system in 1967,

LOOK AND FEEL YOUR BEST THE POPEIL WAY

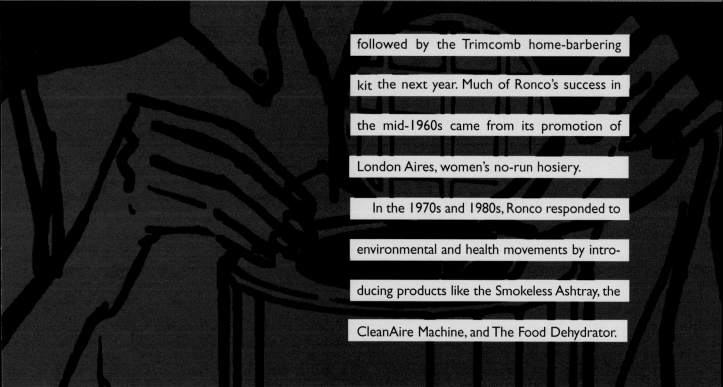

followed by the Trimcomb home-barbering kit the next year. Much of Ronco's success in the mid-1960s came from its promotion of London Aires, women's no-run hosiery.

In the 1970s and 1980s, Ronco responded to environmental and health movements by introducing products like the Smokeless Ashtray, the CleanAire Machine, and The Food Dehydrator.

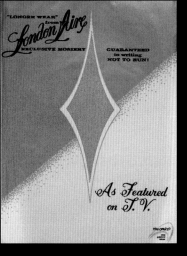

GUARANTEED
IN WRITING
NOT TO RUN

Elegantly Sheer

STEAM MAKES THE DIFFERENCE!

2 minute

Steamset ®

PERSONAL HAIRSETTER

the one and only
hairsetter that conditions
and sets hair
with STEAM ROLLERS

plea

STEAMSET
(POPEIL BROTHERS, 1967)

The idea of creating a device to steam women's hair rollers for a rapid set came after Samuel Popeil observed his wife pressing a shirt with a steam iron. Housed in a high-style pink-and-black plastic steaming box, the Steamset consisted of specially made rollers that could absorb moisture. As a bonus, it came with a plastic face mask that could be placed over the opened box to create a facial steamer and vaporizer.

Get to Know Your TRICOMB

You'll notice one side of the cutting head says, "Shape and Blend" and the other side says "Trim and Thin."

TRIM AND THIN
For tapering or removing small amounts of hair

TRIMCOMB
(POPEIL BROTHERS, 1968)

Trimcomb probably never put any barbershops out of business, but it was still a best-selling gadget for giving haircuts at home. Simple and practical, it consisted of a small handheld comb with a razor blade sandwiched within its teeth. With a little skill and practice, it could trim, thin, and taper by just combing. With a quick flip of the cutting head, the Trimcomb became a shaver that was ideal for sideburn edging, neckline clean-up, or leg grooming.

ROUND FACE • Round faces look somewhat thinner with hair cut close to head at sides,

THE MOD LOOK • The ''Beatle'' cut...very European.

THIN FACE • Fill out a thin face by keeping hair full at the sides.

THE TAPERED NECKLINE • Does away with the straight-line or just-shaved look.

SHAPE AND BLEND
This side is used for removing larger amounts of hair, as well as shaping and blending. It's especially good for doing the back of a man's or boy's hair.

This message is not for barbers. Now, anyone can trim hair and eliminate costly haircuts. If you can comb, you can use Trimcomb. It automatically follows head shape. Just comb. It's that simple. It trims and thins—shapes, blends, and tapers. All you do is comb. Now flip this magic head, and it becomes a shaver that can clean untidy necklines and even sideburns like a barber. You'll love it for grooming feminine legs

SQUARE JAW • Minimize a square jaw by curving hair forward at chin level.

THE TEEN CUT • Natural, easy-going lines that fall easily into place.

NARROW JAW • Hair flipped out at chin level helps to disguise a narrow jaw.

THE YOUNG EXECUTIVE • A true "continental" razor-cut style for the youthful look.

silky smooth. Try it for ten days. Be satisfied or the store will refund your money. Girls, boys, moms, and dads will all use Trimcomb. Get Trimcomb, a styling booklet, supply of blades, and sturdy case, all for $2.99—practically the cost of one haircut.

—Trimcomb commercial, 1968

Ronco ™
Steam-a-way ™
PORTABLE STEAMER
THE NEW, FAST, CONVENIENT WAY TO KEEP YOUR CLOTHING
AND HOUSEHOLD ARTICLES LOOKING TAILORED FRESH.

Made in U.S.A

© 1970 RONCO INC.

UL

STEAM-A-WAY
(RONCO, INC., 1970)

One of Ronco's rare exclusive home products was this portable handheld steamer that could remove wrinkles from any fabric, thus eliminating costly dry cleaning bills. Its compact size made it a nifty travel companion—just like having a valet in your suitcase.

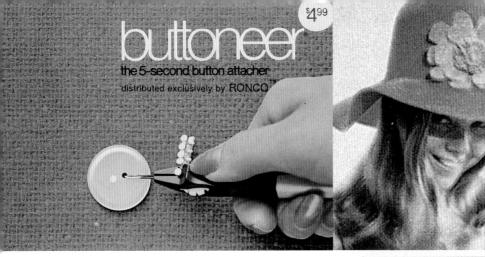

buttoneer

the 5-second button attacher
distributed exclusively by RONCO™

$4⁹⁹

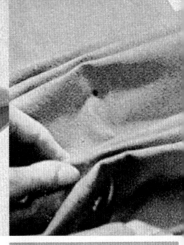

THE BUTTONEER
(DISTRIBUTED BY RONCO TELEPRODUCTS, 1971)

Made by the Dennison Manufacturing Company and distributed by Ronco, the Buttoneer's claim to fame was that it could reattach a button in five seconds with durable plastic brads, thereby eliminating the need to sew. A direct descendant of the Buttoneer's technology are the H-shaped plastic fasteners that stores use to attach price tags to clothing.

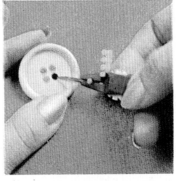

Insert needle through button and fabric ... push handle.

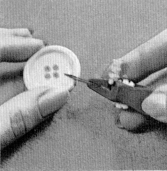

Remove needle; button is attached for good.

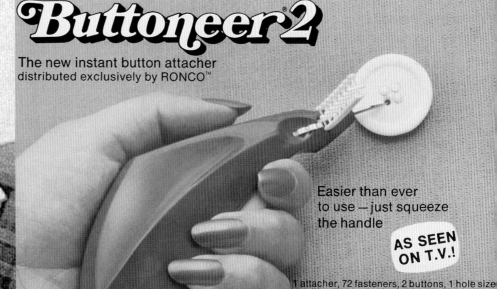

Buttoneer 2

The new instant button attacher
distributed exclusively by RONCO™

Easier than ever to use — just squeeze the handle

AS SEEN ON T.V.!

1 attacher, 72 fasteners, 2 buttons, 1 hole size

(3) VENTED LID

_G_ CHAMBER

LOCKING TAB   **(1)**

TIDIE DRIER
(RONCO TELEPRODUCTS, 1972)

This portable tabletop electric dryer was perfect for drying lingerie, stockings, and other fine hand-washables at the last minute. By slipping the plastic hose and bonnet over its top, the Tidie Drier could be transformed into a handy salon-style hair dryer.

RONCO

Tidie Drier

(2) OUTER COV

(1) LOCKING TAB

I don't think we'll ever run out of ideas. There's always going to be some necessity that you never knew you needed, but you absolutely can't live without.

—Ron Popeil, 1982

AS SEEN ON TV

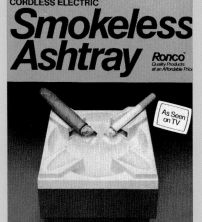

SMOKELESS ASHTRAY
(RONCO TELEPRODUCTS, 1970)

Ronco introduced the Smokeless Ashtray amidst the increase in public awareness regarding environmental issues and the health hazards of smoking. The original model was an ordinary ashtray placed within a tall plastic cylinder that was topped by a cordless electric filtering exhaust fan. Vintage examples of this model often bear burn marks on the side of the cylinder inflicted by inattentive smokers who missed the access opening to the ashtray. It was given a stylish redesign without the overhead cylinder in 1979. A special model for cars was introduced in 1980.

CLEANAIRE MACHINE
(RONCO TELEPRODUCTS, 1982)

Promoted as "the anti-pollution machine," the CleanAire Machine was introduced as an affordable way to remove smoke, pollutants, and odors in the home or office. Retailing for $30—the highest priced Ronco product ever at that time—the CleanAire Machine went into head-to-head competition with similar and more expensive products made by major manufacturers like Norelco and Remington. Its promotion was halted by Ronco's bankruptcy in 1984.

GLH™ formula number 9 hair system

Colored Hair Thickener

Finishing Shield

Hair Cleanser

Trimcomb

GLH FORMULA #9
(RONCO, 1992)

This product's real name is GLH (short for Great Looking Hair) Formula #9, but most people know it as "Hair in a Can." One of Ron Popeil's best-known products of the early 1990s, this powdery spray magically masks bald spots and areas of thinning hair. Popeil had to travel to Australia to secure the rights to manufacture this mysterious substance that actually gives thickness and body to existing hair and washes out with a shampoo. The product has garnered Popeil the best publicity of any of his products and has joined the Veg-O-Matic, Pocket Fisherman, and Mr. Microphone as a classic television-promoted item.

DARK BROWN	MED. BROWN	LIGHT BROWN
AUBURN	SILVER BLACK	SILVER BROWN
BLONDE	WHITE	BLACK

Totes & Handbags

Hats & Caps

Ronco introduced a number of craft-oriented products during the 1970s to reach a younger demographic. The steadily growing interest in handcrafts and recycling since the 1960s created an ideal market for best-selling products like the Bottle and Jar Cutter and the Rhinestone and Stud Setter. Most of the craft products were hand-operated devices

CRAFT FUN FOR THE ENTIRE FAMILY

rendered in colorful plastic by Ronco's design and manufacturing collaborators John S. Doyel and Herman Brickman.

Belts & Accessories

MAKE YOUR OWN PLANTS AT HOME!

•

IT'S LOADS OF FUN!

•

SAVES YOU MONEY TOO!

LARGE WALL PLANTER ▶

Beautify YOUR HOME OR OFFICE WITH "Tropic-Green" PLASTIC PLANTS

ACTUAL ARRANGEMENTS MADE WITH "Tropic-Green" PLASTIC PLANTS

New *Beauty-Rite** Plastic Plant-maker

beautify
your home
with exciting,
life-like
decorator
plants

POPEIL
A PRODUCT

PLASTIC PLANT KIT
(POPEIL BROTHERS, 1957)

At a time when plastic plants were considered new and exotic, Popeil Brothers introduced a kit that could produce "realistic" plastic plants at home. Special liquid plastics were provided for spreading into leaf-shaped metal molds that were to be left to dry on a radiator or warm surface. The finished leaves could be arranged in naturalistic arrangements that never needed watering! The kit was one of Samuel and Raymond Popeil's few ventures into making craft-related products and was a popular item for live-demonstration pitchmen.

SUPERVISION

AS SEEN ON T.V.

Ronco™
bottle & jar cutter
cuts round or square bottles and jars

BOTTLE AND JAR CUTTER
(RONCO TELEPRODUCTS, 1972)

This versatile glass cutter could transform bottles or jars of any shape into drinking glasses, candlesticks, vases, and other decorative and useful household objects.

RHINESTONE AND STUD SETTER
(RONCO TELEPRODUCTS, 1974)

This colorful plastic punch could dress up any kind of cloth, leather, or vinyl with fashion studs and rhinestones, hence its appeal to the fashion- and crafts-minded. The idea folder that accompanied the Setter is a virtual guide to 1970s' fashion.

$\longrightarrow$

A modern hobby craft.
Fun for the whole family.

aquariums

party dishes

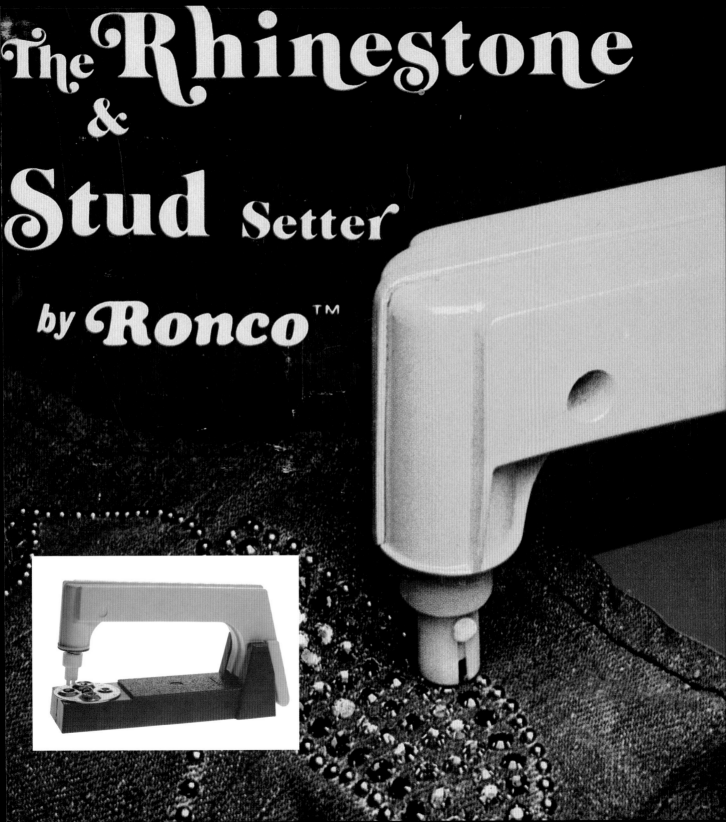

The commercial for Ornamental Ice promised that it "adds elegance to any table, and it's so easy." All the consumer had to do to make any party look like the work of a fine hotel or fancy caterer was fill the rubber molds with water and place them in the home freezer for twenty-four hours.

SPEED TUFTING KIT, FLOWER LOOM
(RONCO TELEPRODUCTS, 1975)

Ronco offered a number of textile handcraft kits in the 1970s, such as the Speed Tufting Kit, which made small rugs and hangings, and the Flower Loom, which made yarn flowers and crocheted circles that could be assembled into afghans, tablecloths, or articles of clothing.

We simply tell you how the product will save you money and time, and we hit you over the head until you know it.

—Ron Popeil, 1982

POTTERY WHEEL
(RONCO TELEPRODUCTS, 1977)

The Pottery Wheel promised consumers that they could make pottery at home just like a professional, but without all the mess and special equipment. Specially formulated clay was included that could be fired in a home oven. No special kilns were needed!

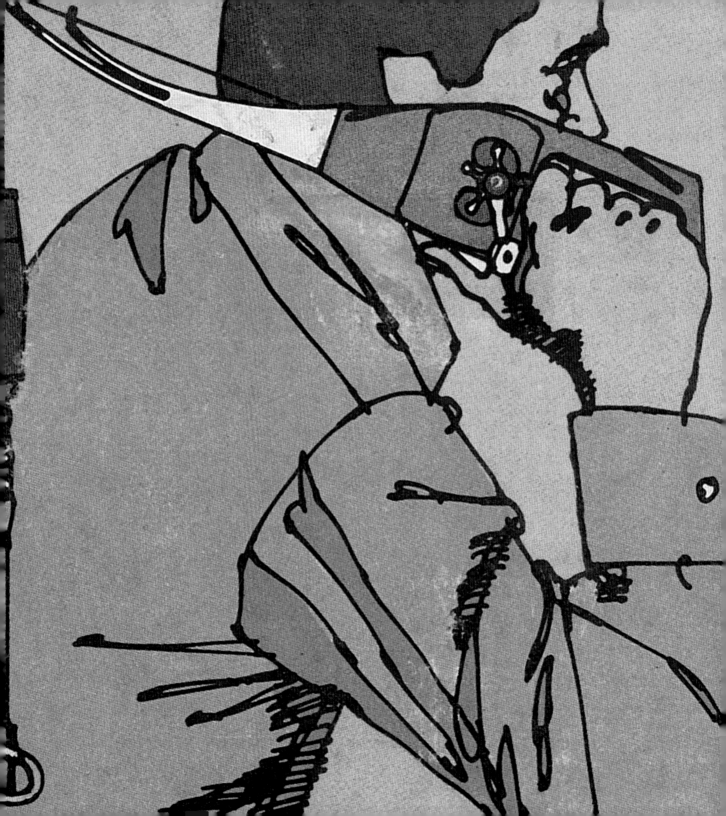

Samuel Popeil was never known as a sportsman or a devotee of the great outdoors, so it came as a surprise to friends and family when he threw himself into developing a portable fishing pole that ultimately became the famous Pocket Fisherman. Inspiration for the product came to Popeil as a result of his nearly getting his eye poked out while waiting for a plane at Chicago's O'Hare airport by a careless child carrying a fishing pole. Angry and in pain from the encounter, the event immediately triggered a personal mission to address the problem in a new and creative way. Back at the Chicago factory, Popeil delved into the project with the single-minded zeal that characterized the development of his other products. The challenge was to create an efficient fishing pole that not only was small, but also could be folded up to fit in one's pocket. Working closely with designer Walter Herbst, Popeil eventually developed a prototype with a pleasingly curved body that contained the reel line

IS THAT A FISHING POLE IN YOUR POCKET?

and a $7\frac{3}{4}$-inch pole of high-strength nylon that folded back neatly when not in use.

Many of Popeil's family and friends looked upon the Pocket Fisherman as a potential business disaster. Expensive and labor-intensive to manufacture, it was ultimately retailed at $19.95—an unusually high price for a television-advertised product. Ron Popeil thought his father was "out of his mind" for charging such a hefty price for a product he believed should retail for $9.99. Another skeptic was designer Walter Herbst, who at one point suggested that Popeil give up the project. Samuel's reply was to the point: "You create 'em...I'll sell 'em."

As usual, Popeil's instincts were literally on the money. Intoduced in 1972, the Pocket Fisherman was a runaway success. The commercial got special air play around Father's Day and Christmas, and it became one of the best known of the Popeil advertisements.

*Truly the NEW Fishing
Invention of the Century*

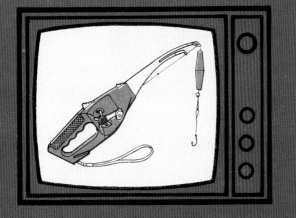

pocket
fisherman*

Spin Casting Outfit

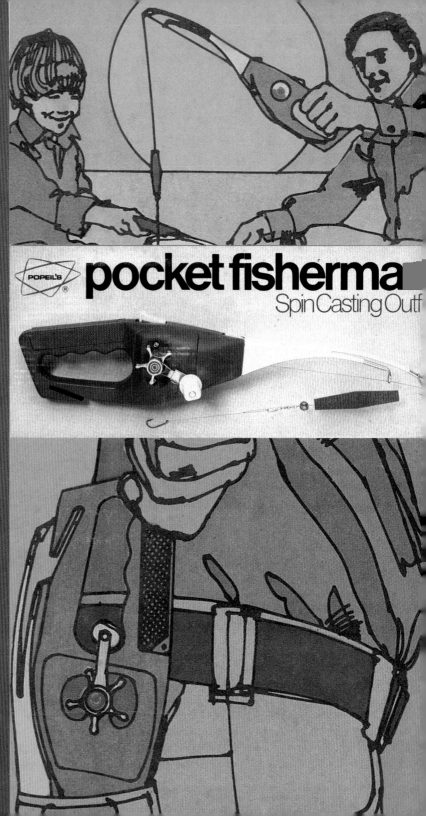

POPEIL'S **pocket fisherma**

Spin Casting Outf

The biggest fishing invention since the hook is Pocket Fisherman. Just imagine yourself landing a bass like this. Pocket Fisherman is so compact, just remove bobber, hook, and sinker from its mini tackle box, lock the rod in place—you're ready to catch fish. Pocket Fisherman is just the right size for ice fishing. It's almost like catching fish in a barrel! Want to make a boy happy? Just give him a Pocket Fisherman. It's so easy to cast! You don't have to be an expert to catch fish. Sooner than

you think, you'll bring in a beauty like this one—and when you do, *hang on tight*! Whether you're a pro or amateur, you'll love Pocket Fisherman. It's quality fishing equipment that can be used with bait or your favorite lure. It really catches fish! It really works, or the store the refunds your money. It's such a great idea! And still only $19.95!

Sold without a hook or bobber, and of a simplified design, the Tadpole was a discounted version of the Pocket Fisherman.

RETRACT-O-NET
(POPEIL BROTHERS, 1977)

The Retract-O-Net worked overtime to provide many uses for its purchasers. It could go from being an easy-to-transport, compact unit to a full-sized net with just a pull on the handle. Live fish could be put into the open net, which could then be retracted to hold them securely. When a special plastic sleeve was slipped over the retracted net, it could serve as an emergency boat paddle.

CAVIAR BAIT KIT
(POPEIL BROTHERS, 1977)

This gadget allowed fishermen to make their own bait from Popeil-provided caviar fish eggs.

THE POPEILS ARE EVERYWHERE!

The Popeils and their products have been permanently enshrined in the annals of American popular culture. Their name, products, and influences can be found everywhere, from television programs to popular music.

The Simpsons: In a 1992 episode of Matt Groening's animated television series *The Simpsons*, Bart Simpson makes trouble with a Mr. Microphone–type device he receives for his birthday. In a 1999 episode of Groening's animated show *Futurama*, Ron Popeil appears as a talking head in a jar, kept alive indefinitely by means of his own inventive technology. Popeil himself provided the voice for the episode.

Dan Aykroyd and *Saturday Night Live*: One of *Saturday Night Live*'s classic comedy skits is Dan Aykroyd's 1976 "advertisement" for the "Bass-O-Matic '76," which liquefied a whole fish "just the way you like it." Other Popeil-style Aykroyd takeoffs included the "Ronco Mohawk Master," essentially two hair clippers joined together but separated by a two-inch gap, that delivered fast and easy mohawk-style haircuts, and the "Ronco Chinch Ranch" for the profitable home raising of chinchillas, which took a swipe at the advertisements that ran in the 1960s through the 1980s that claimed fortunes could be made by raising chinchillas and selling their pelts.

Sneakers: In this 1992 movie starring Robert Redford, a Pocket Fisherman is used as a tool to pull off a high-tech heist. Redford and the Pocket Fisherman were in good company, as the film also featured a line up that included Bass-O-Matic man Dan Aykroyd as well as Sidney Poitier, James Earl Jones, Ben Kingsley, and River Phoenix.

Gallagher and the Sledge-O-Matic: Comedian Gallagher has been smashing assorted fruits and vegetables with a sledgehammer dubbed the "Sledge-O-Matic" in his night club act since 1978. The whacking and splattering is always accompanied by a well-polished Popeil-style pitch incantation.

"Mr. Popeil" by Weird Al Yankovic: Popular music satirist Weird Al Yankovic paid tribute to Popeilania with the release of his 1984 song "Mr. Popeil." Backup singing was provided by Samuel J. Popeil's daughter Lisa, an accomplished vocalist who recorded extensively with Frank Zappa, and has had a prolific career of her own.

"Dodge Veg-O-Matic": How is a much-loved used car that's given up the ghost like a Veg-O-Matic? Jonathan Richman and the Modern Lovers somehow tied the two together in the 1977-released song "Dodge Veg-O-Matic."

"Vegematic" by Steve Goodman: The plight of a person compelled to buy everything advertised on television was the subject of this 1983 Steve Goodman song written in collaboration with satirist Shel Silverstein and Mike Smith.

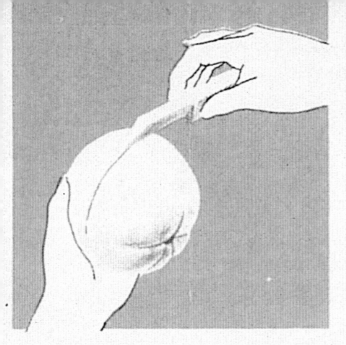
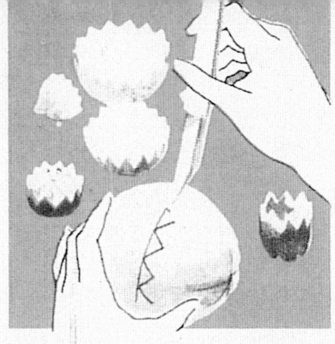

Harlequin Design—For Melons, Grapefruit, Lemons, Oranges, Tomatoes, Peppers, Hard-Boiled Eggs, etc.: Circle with Fancy Cut Marker (No. 6) for guide line. Pierce with Fancy Cutter (No. 7) along guide line so that V's touch.

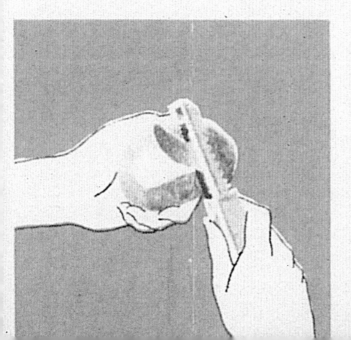
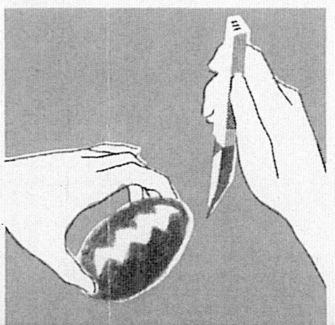

COOK

As Popeil Brothers and Ronco diversified their line of products to include everything from hair cutters to record vacuums, they still kept food-processing appliances as an important part of their television lineup. As was part of their pitching heritage, they continued in their never-ending search to find a new and better way to shred cabbage or to create products that would make customers sit up, take

MIRACLES IN YOUR KITCHEN

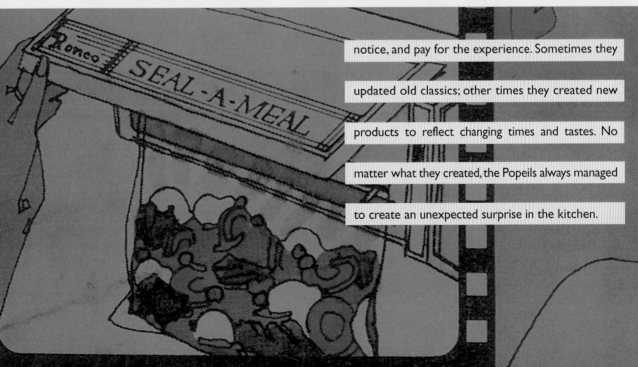

SEAL

notice, and pay for the experience. Sometimes they updated old classics; other times they created new products to reflect changing times and tastes. No matter what they created, the Popeils always managed to create an unexpected surprise in the kitchen.

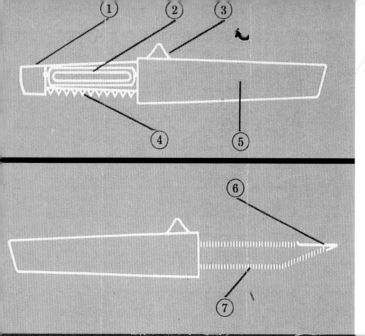

It almost seems as if Samuel Popeil felt compelled to make the tiny Food Glamorizer do a record number of kitchen chores, thus giving literal meaning to the phrase "does the work of a whole drawerful of appliances." This product could perform thirteen functions: harlequin-cut fruit; make carrot curls; peel fruits and vegetables; remove eyes from potatoes; decorate baked potatoes; peel carrots; shred cabbage; make decorative radish roses; make orange- or lemon-peel twists for mixed drinks; cut cheese strips; remove strings from celery; make decorative lemon wheels; and carve pumpkins.

*kitchen magician**
FOOD GLAMORIZER

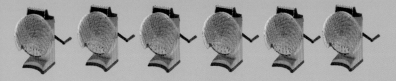

KITCHEN MAGICIAN
(POPEIL BROTHERS, 1970)

With its distinctive 1970s' styling and green plastic housing, the Kitchen Magician was touted as a versatile and attractive addition to any modern kitchen. Special "conveyor action" faultlessly guided any kind of food through its interchangeable steel cutting blades. The name "Kitchen Magician" was recycled from a term used in conjunction with Popeil Brothers' earlier "Food Glamorizer."

COOK

SEAL

Ronco
SEAL-A-MEAL

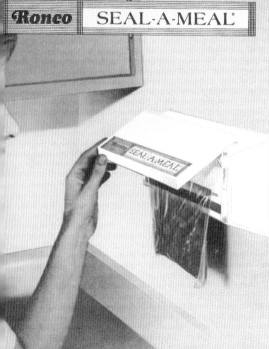

Ronco SEAL-A-MEAL

RECIPE AND INSTRUCTION BOOK

SEAL-A-MEAL
(DISTRIBUTED BY RONCO TELEPRODUCTS, 1971)

The popular Seal-A-Meal was briefly sold by Ronco on behalf of the Dazey Corporation of Kansas City. Similar devices which heat-seal foods in plastic bags are still on the market today.

STORE

HEAT

SERVE

salad Spinner *and Whipper* by *Ronco*™

Giant Capacity 8 salad servings

As seen on **TV**

Presco'lator™ *COFFEE & TEA MAKER* by *Ronco*™

As seen on TV

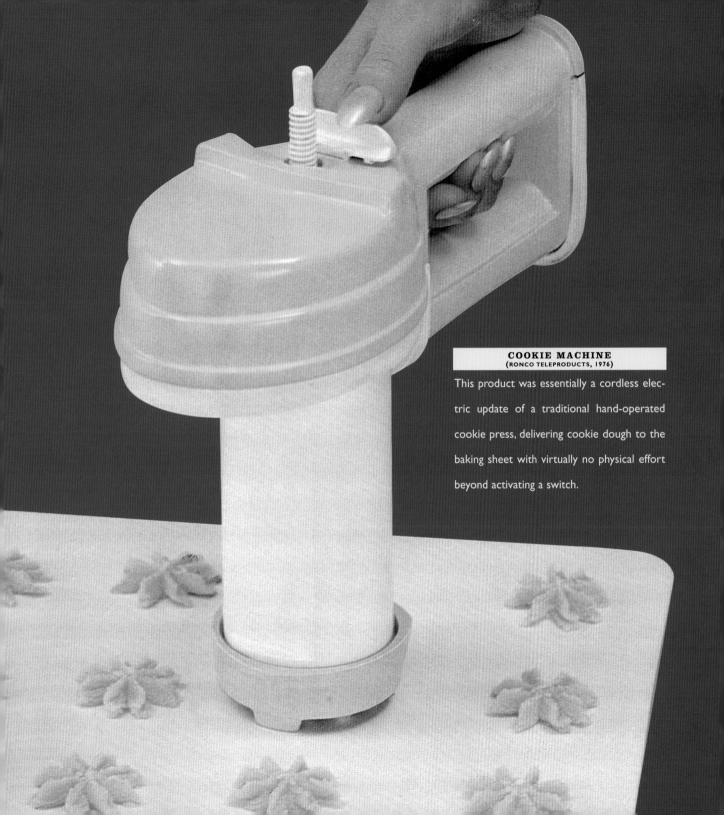

COOKIE MACHINE
(RONCO TELEPRODUCTS, 1976)

This product was essentially a cordless electric update of a traditional hand-operated cookie press, delivering cookie dough to the baking sheet with virtually no physical effort beyond activating a switch.

POTATO CHIP MACHINE
(RONCO TELEPRODUCTS, 1977)

In concept, this device was a mechanized version of the traditional pitchman's spiral slicer, which could twirl vegetables into a spiraling coil. For promotional purposes, this machine was given a more specific identity as a home potato chip maker, even though it could also slice and shred a wide variety of foods.

FOOD DEHYDRATOR
(RONCO, INC., 1979)

Ron Popeil has given special attention to improving and redesigning the Ronco Food Dehydrator since its introduction in 1979. In return, the product has proved to be good to Ron Popeil, as it was his best-selling item in the mid-1980s when the bankruptcy of Ronco

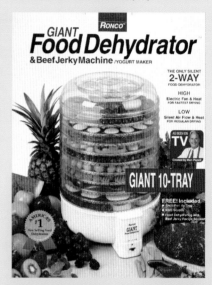

Teleproducts put him back on the live-demonstration fair circuit. It was also the product that marked his return to television and was the subject of his first infomercial in the early 1990s. Devices for dehydrating foods and making yogurt were commonplace during this period, but the Ronco version was one of the most popular due to its affordable price.

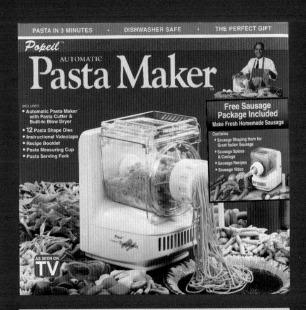

AUTOMATIC PASTA MAKER
(POPEIL PASTA PRODUCTS INC., 1994)

Like most of Ron Popeil's 1990s' products, the Automatic Pasta Maker was sold on television via extended audience participation infomercials. The machine makes any pasta shape: simply pour raw ingredients into the bowl and turn it on. In the Popeil tradition of creating a product that performs more than one function, it also can be used as a sausage maker.

GRIP SPATULA
(RONCO ENTERPRISES, 1995)

Just as his father had devised the Automatic Egg Turner in 1948, Ron Popeil put his own spin on the ordinary spatula by inventing a plastic version that gripped items as it flipped them.

SET IT . . . AND FORGET IT!
(SHOWTIME ROTISSERIE (RONCO, INC., 1998)

Forty-two years after twenty-one-year-old Ron Popeil first stood before the cameras to demonstrate the Chop-O-Matic, he appeared again to pitch his Showtime Rotisserie. Much had transpired in television, marketing, and his own life between the two commercials, yet there was a comfortable continuity between the two. In both advertisements, Popeil demonstrated that he was the master of the pitch and that time had improved rather than diminished his ability to sell a product.

Large-scale home rotisseries had been available for decades, but the Showtime Rotisserie was designed to fit in compact kitchens, was easier to use, and saved electricity. Origins of the Showtime Rotisserie can be found in the half-hour commercials produced in the early 1950s for the Roto-Broil rotisserie. Presented in the form of a cooking show, it starred Ron Popeil's cousin Lester Morris (son of his uncle, Nat Morris, see Introduction), who demonstrated such features as the "Slide-O-Matic" glass door that slid under the unit and a heated surface at the top for additional cooking space.

Similar features found their way into the Showtime Rotisserie, but most of the new rotisserie's compact, easy-to-use features evolved under Ron Popeil's direction for the 1990s' kitchen. Even though Popeil worked with longtime design collaborator Alan Backus and other consultants in developing the Showtime Rotisserie, many of its features and innovations were the result of Popeil's own trial-and-error experimentation in the kitchen of his Beverly Hills home. In the infomercial, Popeil states that the Showtime Rotisserie was his greatest invention. With nearly three million sold to date, his claim seems justly verified—well, at least until his next invention comes along.

OVERSIZED BOX TO PROTECT CONTENTS
ROTISSERIE IS NO WIDER THAN A TOASTER OVEN

PLATINUM EDITION

Ronco

Showtime™

ROTISSERIE & BBQ

AS SEEN ON TV
Created by Ron Popeil

- Great for 1-2 People and Perfect for Large Families and Parties!
- The Perfect Mother's Day, Father's Day, Christmas, Wedding and Holiday Gift
- Rotisserie up to a 15 lb. Turkey
- Finally - A BBQ That's Really Easy to Clean Up!

FREE BBQ GLOVES INCLUDED FOR YOUR CONVENIENCE

"Cut the Fat" ... Naturally

AUTOMATIC INFRA-RED COMPLETE ELECTRIC KITCHEN

ROTO-BROIL "400" RIVIERA

ROTO-BROIL CUSTOM "400" and BAK-A-TRAY

RON POPEIL: How much are they and where can you get them? You all want to know—right?

AUDIENCE: Right!

RON POPEIL: I was looking at some mail-order catalogs and I tell ya, they have rotisserie barbecues in here ranging anywhere from a hundred and fifty dollars up to two thousand dollars!

AUDIENCE: Oooohhhh...

RON POPEIL: You're not going to have to spend two thousand dollars, or a thousand dollars for my product—in fact, when you buy them in retail stores they're going to come with this very fancy package over here—they're gonna sell for three hundred and nineteen dollars—and believe me, they're worth three hundred and nineteen dollars for all the work they do. You're not going to spend around three hundred and twenty dollars here, you're not going to spend three hundred, not two ninety or

two eighty, not two seventy, not two twenty, not even two hundred, not a hundred and ninety or a hundred and eighty, and not even a hundred and seventy dollars, like you may all be thinking. If you call the toll-free number now, and tell a friend about it, all you'll spend for this fabulous machine is just four easy payments of thirty-nine dollars and ninety-five cents.

AUDIENCE: (Applause).

RON POPEIL: Everybody that calls right now is going to get the steam and heating tray absolutely free. You can do all your

vegetables, keeps two vegetables piping hot for six or eight people while the food is rotating on the inside. You also get your basket—it does all your salmon steaks, your sirloin steaks, nine quarter-pound hamburgers. You're going to get that non-stick basket with it. You get food ties, you get six shish kabob rods to do your sausages, hot dogs, and kabobs. You get your platform. You also get a pair of barbecue gloves. You get the flavor injector. A hundred dollars' worth of coupons, and of course, if you're buying it as a gift for someone—and it makes a fabulous holiday gift—a gift for anybody and everybody—you get a

booklet with instructions and recipes and you also get a videocassette so your friends can't make any mistakes when they use the machine. This whole package is over a five-hundred-dollar value, and all it costs you here—if you call the toll-free number right now—is just four easy payments of thirty-nine dollars and ninety-five cents. Please call the toll-free number— thank you—you'll be glad you did.

AUDIENCE: (Applause).

Acknowledgments

Capturing the Popeil story between the covers of a book was a challenging task. While the Popeils are well-known icons of American popular culture, their work was largely done for the moment, with little, if any, thought given to documenting their achievements for posterity. Without extensive written records, researching their legacy proved to be as ethereal as a pitchman's spiel at a county fair, or the seductive power of television advertising. This book would not have been possible without the help of Popeil family members, as well as friends and coworkers who generously took the time to fill in the Popeil puzzle to create a complete and vivid picture.

My earliest contact was Ron Popeil himself, who nearly eight years ago answered my letter regarding the design aspects of early Popeil products with a friendly and informative phone call. He patiently brought me back to earth whenever I loftily interpreted product-design aesthetics which were in reality the result of practical business decisions. "That's how you historians get fooled," he warned—good advice that I have kept in mind throughout this project. He has continued to provide valuable assistance over the years, as have his associates Gina Wallman and Jan Gildersleeve.

I'm especially thankful for my contact with Samuel Popeil's daughters and relatives. Pamela Popeil and her husband, Will, not only have been helpful, but also have become friends in the process. Lisa Popeil generously turned over her notes for a never-realized television documentary and encouraged me to carry on the work. My thanks, too, to Arnold "The Knife" Morris, who provided many informative and entertaining conversations about the amazing Morris relatives in Asbury Park.

Friends and business associates have also been generous with their help. Ronco co-founder Mel Korey astounded me with his abilities of almost total recall, even remembering to the penny the wholesale price of a Veg-O-Matic in 1964. S. J. Popeil's friend and patent attorney, Jack Dominik, shared many wonderful facts and stories. Popeil Brothers' reliable financial wizard Phil Rootberg provided an insider's perspective to the business side of the story, while Alvin Eicoff shared insights on producing pitch-style television advertisements in the 1950s, including his pioneering commercial for Popeil Brothers' Chop-O-Matic in 1956.

My interest in the product design of Popeil merchandise was enhanced by my contact with longtime Popeil Brothers designer Walter Herbst, and Ronco's first custom product designer, John S. Doyel. Both gave flair and style to the products and my story. Also helpful was John Doyel's partner and manufacturing associate, Herman Brickman.

I was deeply honored when Chicago photography legend David R. Philips offered to create the illustrations for the book. It made me uneasy to have such a noted photographer focus his expertise and equipment on my humble Veg-O-Matics, but the resulting images and the camaraderie we enjoyed in making them was an unforgettable experience.

It would not be enough to thank Joseph Leonardi for guiding me through the legal mysteries of creating a book. First and foremost, he has been a good friend and sounding board throughout the entire project. Also, many thanks to my friend Shirli Dixon-Nelson of the Blues Heaven Foundation for her help and support on behalf of this book.

Considerable help and support was offered by Vicki Matranga, whose extensive research into the design history of home products was pioneering for its time and is still vital today. Helpful guidance in preparing this book also came from John Phillips and Charlie Koenen.

The archives of The Museum of Broadcast Communications in Chicago have been invaluable for providing sources for early commercials, especially through the guidance of Dan Wingate. Special thanks are also due to J. Fred MacDonald for access to original commercials from his film archive.

Many thanks to Elizabeth Sullivan, senior editor at Rizzoli, who had faith in the idea of the book and the patience and perseverance to see it through, and to assistant editor Signe Bergstrom for her attentiveness and hard work. Also, thanks to Kay Schuckhart whose amazing design gave the Popeil saga a presence and voice like nobody else could..

I never fully understood why writers gave such effusive thanks to their spouses in book acknowledgments, until my wife, Barbara Koenen, showed me why—and then some.

Select Bibliography

INTERVIEWS

Brickman, Herman. Telephone interview with author. May 2000.

Dominik, Jack, E. Telephone interviews with author. November 1999 and March 2000.

Doyel, John. Interview with author. April 2000.

Herbst, Walter. Telephone interviews with author. October 1999 and April 2001.

Korey, Mel. Telephone interview with author. August 2000.

Morris, Arnold. Telephone interview with author. April 2000.

Popeil, Lisa. Telephone interview with author. November 1999.

Popeil, Pamela. Telephone interviews and e-mail communications with author beginning
    November 1999 through December 2000.

Popeil, Ronald, M. Telephone interview with author. February 1996.

Rootberg, Phil. Interview with author. July 2000.

BOOKS

Eicoff, Al, and Alvin Eicoff. *Direct Marketing through Broadcast Media.*
    Lincolnwood, Ill.: NTC Business Books, 1995.

Popeil, Ron, with Jefferson Graham. *The Salesman of the Century.*
    New York: Delacorte Press, 1995.

NEWSPAPERS AND PERIODICALS

Butler, Jean. "Introducing the Incredible Ron Popeil and His Miracle Marketing."
    The Chicagoan, October 1973.

Dretzka, Gary. "Master of the Infomercial." *Chicago Tribune*, March 3, 1999.

Dunlap, David W. "But, Wait! You Mean There's More?" *The New York Times*,
    November 11, 1999.

Elsner, David M. "Gadget King Popeil Sees Empire Crumble." *Chicago Tribune*,
    September 12, 1979, Section 4, page 1.

Fields, Teri. "TV's Pushy Peddlers." *US*, September 28, 1982.

Gladwell, Malcolm. "The Pitchman." *The New Yorker*, October 30, 2000.

Greenberg, Herb. "Ronco Learns Peril of Sailing Uncharted Seas." *Chicago Tribune*,
    January 22, 1984.

Schultz, Susy. "Samuel Popeil, 69; Pocket Fisherman Made Him Famous." *Chicago Sun-Times*, July 20, 1984.

Index

About the Author

TIMOTHY SAMUELSON, curator of architecture and design at the Chicago Historical Society, is an eminent architectural historian who specializes in the work of Louis Sullivan. A former Loeb Fellow at the Harvard University Graduate School of Design, Samuelson has written extensively on architecture, history, and design, and has done extensive consulting and curatorial work for the country's major fine arts institutions.

A collector of Popeil and Ronco products for ten years, Samuelson has assembled the country's most comprehensive archive of materials relating to these well-known companies. His interest in the subject has been covered in feature articles in *The New York Times*, *Chicago Sun-Times*, *Boston Globe*, *The New Yorker*, *Chicago* magazine, and other publications. He has also done considerable radio and television interviews on the subject. He lives in Chicago, Illinois.